Philip

Shiv

Methuen Drama

Published by Methuen Drama 2012

Methuen Drama, an imprint of Bloomsbury Publishing Plc

1 3 5 7 9 10 8 6 4 2

Methuen Drama
Bloomsbury Publishing Plc
50 Bedford Square
London WC1B 3DP
www.methuendrama.com

First published by Methuen Drama in 2012

ISBN 978 1 408 17259 9

A CIP catalogue record for this book is available from the British Library

Available in the USA from Bloomsbury Academic & Professional, 175 Fifth Avenue/3rd Floor, New York, NY 10010. www.BloomsburyAcademicUSA.com

Typeset by Mark Heslington Ltd, Scarborough, North Yorkshire
Printed and bound in Great Britain by CPI Group (UK) Ltd, Croydon CR0 4YY

This book is produced using paper that is made from wood grown in managed, sustainable forests. It is natural, renewable and recyclable. The logging and manufacturing processes conform to the environmental regulations of the country of origin.

Aron Rollin and Caitlin Albery Beavan
for Moya Productions present

Shivered

by Philip Ridley

First performance on Wednesday 7 March at the Southwark Playhouse Theatre, London.

Supported by the Stage One Bursary Scheme for New Producers

stage one
INVESTING IN THEATRE

Shivered
by Philip Ridley

Cast (in order of appearance)

Alec	Robbie Jarvis
Ryan	Joseph Drake
Jack	Josh Williams
Lyn	Olivia Poulet
Gordy	Andrew Hawley
Evie	Amanda Daniels
Mikey	Simon Lenagan

Director	Russell Bolam
Designer	Anthony Lamble
Lighting	Richard Howell
Sound	Tom Gibbons
Assistant Director	Ross Drury
Fight Direction	Malcolm Ranson
Movement	Anna Morrissey
Casting	Sophie Falkner & Charlotte Sutton

Production Manager	Matt Noddings
Company Stage Manager	Peta Dyce
Assistant Stage Manager	Katie Munro Farlie

THE COMPANY

Amanda Daniels (Evie)

Amanda's work in theatre includes: *Wild Horses* (Theatre503), *Days Of Significance* (RSC), *The Winter's Tale* (RSC), *Pericles* (RSC), *13 Grape Street* (Pleasance Theatre), *Third Finger, Left Hand* (Theatre Royal York, New End Theatre, Assembly Rooms), *Tartuffe* (Cockpit Theatre), *The Accrington Pals* (Pentameters), *April in Paris* (Man in the Moon), *A Midsummer Night's Dream* (Grange Court).

TV includes: *Doctors, Casualty, Doc Martin, Holby City, Sea of Souls, Marital Harmony, Silent Witness, The Bill, Rosemary & Thyme, Auf Wiedersehen, Pet.*

Film includes: *Balloon Man, Paroxetine, A Woman Spawned.*

Joseph Drake (Ryan)

Joseph trained at Bristol Old Vic Theatre School.

His work in theatre includes: *The Lion in Winter* (Theatre Royal Haymarket), *Rattigan's Njinsky, Deep Blue Sea* (Chichester Festival Theatre), *Kingdom Of Earth* (The Print Room), *Vernon God Little* (The Young Vic).

Andrew Hawley (Gordy)

Andrew's work in theatre includes: *All The Little Things We Crushed* (Almeida Theatre), *The History Boys* (UK Tour and Wyndhams Theatre), *Pushing Up Poppies* (Venue 13, Edinburgh), *Iphigenia* (Crucible Theatre).

TV includes: *The Syndicate, Cricklewood Greats, Borgia, Lewis, Wuthering Heights.*

Film includes: *Snow White and The Huntsman, A Night In The Woods, Age of Heroes, A Spanking in Paradise, Dust, The Strays* (short).

Robbie Jarvis (Alec)

Robbie's work in theatre includes: *The Thing About Haverstock* (The Roundhouse), *Two Days In Prison Three Days At Home* (Tristan Bates Theatre), *Lucy, Faliraki, The Greek Tragedy* (National Youth Theatre).

TV includes: *Upstairs, Downstairs, Trial and Retribution, Waking the Dead, The Real Midnight Express, Genie in the House.*

Film includes: *Harry Potter and the Order Of The Phoenix, Full Firearms, The History Boys, Coming Back, The Space You Leave.*

Simon Lenagan (Mikey)
Simon trained at Webber Douglas Academy & Birmingham University.

His work in theatre includes: *Normal* (The Union Theatre), *The Penetrator* (Old Red Lion), *Macbeth* (Westcliff), *The Way Of The World* (Royal Exchange), *Stand-Up* (Old Red Lion/ Edinburgh Fringe), *Room At The Top* (King's Head), *The Greenhouse* (Riverside Studios), *The Long And The Short And The Tall* (Albery Theatre), *Punch Junkies* (Brixton Shaw Theatre).

TV includes: *Survivors, The Palace, Holby Blue, The Time Of Your Life, Spooks, Heartbeat, Holby City, May 33rd, The Brief, Coronation Street, Messiah II, Outside The Rules, Monarch Of The Glen, Other People's Children, This Is Personal – The Hunt For The Yorkshire Ripper, Pure Wickedness, Babes In The Wood, The Grand.*

Film includes: *Born Of War, WMD, Run, Fatboy, Run, Basic Instinct 2: Risk Addiction, Passer By, Bring Me Your Love* (short), *Pear Shaped* (short), *Divine Intervention* (short).

Olivia Poulet (Lyn)
Olivia's work in theatre includes: *Top Girls* (ATG), *A Voyage Round My Father* (Salisbury Playhouse), *Fiasco* (Soho Theatre), *The Queef of Terence* (Pleasance Dome Edinburgh), *Bird Flu Diaries* (The Pleasance Edinburgh), *Map of the Heart* (Salisbury Playhouse), *Major Barbara* (Royal Exchange Manchester), *The Lesson* (King's Head), *The School for Scandal* (Derby Playhouse), *Age, Sex, Location* (Lyric Theatre).

TV includes: *Without You, Dappers, Margot and Mez, Sherlock, The Thick Of It, Margaret, Secret Diary of a Call Girl, Outnumbered, Whatever Love Means, Friends and Crocodiles, Love Soup, The Rotters Club, Inspector Lynley, Silent Witness, Teachers, The Bill, Acorn Antiques.*

Film includes: *In the Loop, Day of the Flowers, Heroes and Villains, Killing Me Softly, Stalking Ben Chadz* (short).

Josh Williams (Jack)

Josh's work in theatre includes: *Lord of the Flies* (Regent's Park open Air Theatre), *Our Private Life* (Royal Court), *Arlo* (Southwark Playhouse).

TV includes: *Holby City*.

Russell Bolam (Director)

Russell's work in theatre includes: *Alfred* (Vineyard Theatre), *The Road to Mecca*, *The Roman Bath* (Arcola Theatre), *Captain Oates' Left Stock* (Finborough Theatre), *Fourplay*, *Three More Sleepless Nights* (Tristan Bates Theatre), *The Physicists* (Aphra Studio). He is a former assistant director at the Royal Shakespeare Company, Bristol Old Vic and The Old Vic.

Russell teaches improvisation at Bristol Old Vic Theatre School, is a visiting director of Shakespeare at RWCMD and visiting practitioner at Kent University. He is the Artistic Director of Green for Go Theatre Company.

Ross Drury (Assistant Director)

Ross trained at East 15 Acting School. His work in theatre includes: *Cut Throat* (Teatro Technis), *A Doll's House* (West Sussex County Youth Theatre), *The Shape Of Things* (Ropetackle Arts Centre), *4.48 Psychosis* (Stephen Joseph/Hull Truck), *A Streetcar Named Desire* (The Basement, Brighton). He assisted Edward Bond on *The Fool* (Cock Tavern) and spent two seasons with the national touring clowning troupe – The Pantaloons.

Ross is the literary manager of MSFT productions and completed the National Theatre directors course 2011. He is also the Artistic Director of Brendan's Boat theatre company.

Peta Dyce (Stage Manager)

Peta's work in theatre includes: *Count Oelerland* (The Arcola/The White Bear), *Howl's Moving Castle*, *The Taming Of The Shrew* (Southwark Playhouse), *The Musical Of Musicals*, *Girlfriends* (Ye Old Rose And Crown Theatre), *Online Courting* (The Hen And Chickens), *Holding Hands At Paschendale* (The White Bear), *I Am Jack*

(Regional Tour), *Flano Fest* (Q Theatre), *Kiss Me Like You Mean It.* (Tamarama Rock Surfers).

Tom Gibbons (Sound)
Tom trained at Central School of Speech and Drama.

Tom's work in theatre includes: *Island* (National Theatre, Tour), *Romeo and Juliet* (Headlong, Tour), *Disco Pigs* (Young Vic), *Dead Heavy Fantastic* (Liverpool Everyman), *Plenty* (Crucible Studio, Sheffield), *Encourage The Others* (Almeida), *Love Love Love*, (Royal Court, Tour), *Wasted* (Paines Plough, Tour), *Chalet Lines, The Knowledge, Little Platoons, 50 Ways To Leave Your Lover, 50 Ways To Leave Your Lover@ Xmas* (Bush Theatre), *Faith, Hope and Charity, The Hostage, Toad* (Southwark Playhouse), *Sold* (503), *The Chairs* (Ustinov Bath), *The Country, The Road To Mecca, The Roman Bath, 1936, The Shawl* (Arcola), *Bagpuss, Everything Must Go, Soho Streets* (Soho Theatre), *The Machine Gunners* (Polka), *Holes* (New Wimbledon Studio), *Terror Tales* (Hampstead Studio), *Faustus* (Watford Palace, Tour), *Faithless Bitches* (Courtyard), *FAT* (The Oval House, Tour), *Just Me Bell* (Graeae, Tour), *Fanta Orange, Blue Heaven* (Finborough), *Pitching In* (Latitude Festival), *US Love Bites* (Old Red Lion, Tristan Bates), *Pendulum* (Jermyn Street). As **Associate Designer** work includes *The Aliens, Broken Space Season* (Bush Theatre)

Tom is resident sound designer for the international physical theatre company Parrot {in the} Tank.

Richard Howell (Lighting Designer)
Richard's work in theatre includes: *Les Parents Terribles* (Donmar/ Trafalgar), *Lettice and Lovage, Great Expectations, Single Spies, Heroes* (Watermill), *Snake in the Grass, Uncle Vanya* (Print Room), *The Table* (Blind Summit Tour), *The Swallowing Dark* (Liverpool / Theatre 503), *Orpheus Underground/Our Days of Rage* (NYT), *The Hairy Ape, Tagore's Women, Faith, Hope and Charity* (Southwark), *.45* (Hampstead), *Romeo and Juliet* (York/Tour), *Wolves at the Window* (Arcola/New York), *The Car Cemetery* (Gate), *Angry Young Man* (Trafalgar 2), *Twelfth Night, Much Ado About Nothing* (Ripley Castle).

Opera includes work for Opera Up Close, Royal College of Music, Guildhall and Clonter Opera. Ballet includes work for London Children's Ballet.

Anthony Lamble (Designer)

Anthony's work in theatre includes: *The Passing, The East Pier, Bookworms, The Comedy of Errors, The Playboy of the Western World* (Abbey Dublin), *For Once* (Pentabus/Hampstead/Traverse), *Relatively Speaking* (Watermill), *Much Ado About Nothing, Twelfth Night* (Ludlow), *Rum & Coca Cola* (ETT/WYP/Talawa), *Bedroom Farce* (WYP), *Comedians* (Lyric), *Loot* (Tricycle), *Romeo and Juliet* (Globe/tour), *The English Game* (Headlong), *The Entertainer* (Old Vic), *Someone Who'll Watch Over Me* (West End), *The Price* (West End/Tricycle/tour), *The Caucasian Chalk Circle, Translations, Sing Yer Heart Out for the Lads, A Midsummer Night's Dream, As You Like It* (National), Numerous productions for the RSC, Royal Court, Menier, OSC, Bush, Chichester, Sheffield, Shared Experience, Coventry Belgrade.

Dance includes work for English National Ballet.

Opera includes work for English National Opera and the Royal Opera House.

Film includes: *The Secret Audience.*

Anna Morrissey (Movement)

Anna's work in theatre includes: *Marat/Sade* (RSC), *Dunsinane* (National Theatre of Scotland/RSC), *Bus Stop* (New Vic Theatre), *My Dad's A Birdman* (Young Vic), *Caledonia* (National Theatre of Scotland), *The Comedy of Errors* (Royal Exchange Theatre), *Antony and Cleopatra, The Grain Store, The Drunks, The Tragedy of Thomas Hobbes, I'll Be the Devil, Cordelia Dream* (RSC), *Hanover Square* (Finborough Theatre), *101 Dalmatians* (Northampton Theatre Royal), *Dr Faustus* (Resolution! The Place), *Restoration* (Headlong Theatre), *Mother Courage* (English Touring Theatre), *On The Record* (Arcola Theatre), *The Tempest, A Warwickshire Testimony, As You Like It, Macbeth* (Bridge House Theatre), *Timon of Athens* (RSC/Cardboard Citizens), *Taming of the Shrew* (Creation Theatre Co.), *Richard III* (Cambridge Arts Theatre), *Hamlet* (Cliffords Tower, York), *The Arab-Israeli*

Cookbook (Tricycle Theatre), *Human Rites* (Southwark Playhouse), *Julius Caesar* (Menier Chocolate Factory), *Tamburlaine the Great* (Rose Theatre).

Opera includes: *Orpheus in the Underworld,* (Scottish Opera), *Hansel and Gretel* (Opera North), *The Barber of Seville, Manon Lescaut* (Opera Holland Park).

Matt Noddings (Production Manager)
Matt's work in theatre includes: *Top Girls* (National Tour), *Beasts and Beauties* (Hampstead Theatre), Crazy For You (Novello Theatre), *Plenty* (Sheffield Crucible), *Love, Love, Love* (National tour), *Pressure Drop* (Wellcome Collection), *1984* (BAC/National tour), *Sunset Boulevard* (Comedy Theatre) *Adolf Hitler: My Part In His Downfall* (National Tour), *Edward Gant's Amazing Feats Of Loneliness* (National Tour).

Matt has been the resident production manager at the Regent's Park Open Theatre since 2010. Matt was previously resident production manager at the Soho Theatre and Theatre Royal York.

Malcolm Ranson (Fight Director)
Malcolm's work in theatre includes: *Not About Nightingales, Oklahoma, Cyrano The Musical, Les Liaisons Dangereuses* and *Les Miserables* (all Broadway productions), *The Plantagenets, The Venetian Twins, The Lion The Witch And The Wardrobe, Hamlet, Romeo And Juliet, Comedy Of Errors, Days Of Significance, King Lear, Taming Of The Shrew* and *The Gods Weep* (RSC), *Oklahoma!, A Streetcar Named Desire, Coast Of Utopia, Dinner, The Relapse* and *Private Lives* (National Theatre), *The War Of The Roses, As You Like It* and *Anthony and Cleopatra* (The English Shakespeare Company), *Singin' in the Rain, When We Are Married, Sister Act, Bombay Dreams, Noises Off, Arsenic & Old Lace, Cat On A Hot Tin Roof, Les Miserables, Woman In White* and *See How They Run* (all West End productions).

Opera includes: *Carmen, Faust* and *Force Of Destiny* (English National Opera), *Sophie's Choice* (Royal Opera House).

TV includes: *Casualty, By The Sword Divided, Black Adder.*

Film includes: *Oklahoma!, Twelfth Night, Edward II, Feast Of July.*

Philip Ridley (Writer)

Philip was born in the East End of London and studied painting at St Martin's School of Art. As well as three books for adults – and the highly acclaimed screenplay for the feature film *The Krays* (winner of the *Evening Standard* Best Film of the Year Award) – he has written eight previous adult stage plays: *The Pitchfork Disney*, the multi-award-winning *The Fastest Clock in the Universe*, *Ghost from a Perfect Place*, *Vincent River*, the highly controversial *Mercury Fur*, *Leaves of Glass*, *Piranha Heights* and *Tender Napalm* (nominated for the London Fringe Best Play Award), plus several plays for young people: *Karamazoo*, *Fairytaleheart*, *Moonfleece*, *Sparkleshark* and *Brokenville* (collectively known as *The Storyteller Sequence*). He has also written books for children, including *Scribbleboy* (shortlisted for the Carnegie Medal), *Kasper in the Glitter* (nominated for the Whitbread Prize), *Mighty Fizz Chilla* (shortlisted for the *Blue Peter* Book of the Year Award), and the bestseller *Krindlekrax* (winner of the Smarties Prize). He has also directed three feature films from his own screenplays: *The Reflecting Skin* – winner of eleven international awards (including the prestigious George Sadoul Prize) – *The Passion of Darkly Noon* (winner of the Best Director Prize at the Porto Film Festival) and *Heartless* (winner of the Silver Méliès Award for Best Fantasy Film). For the latter two films, Philip co-wrote a number of original songs, one of which, 'Who Will Love Me Now?' (performed by PJ Harvey) was voted BBC Radio 1's Top Film Song of 1998 and has since been covered by the techno-house band Suncreem (as 'Please Save Me'), becoming a cult hit in clubs. In 2010 Philip, along with song-writing collaborator Nick Bicât, formed the music group Dreamskin Cradle and their first album, *Songs from Grimm*, is available on iTunes, Amazon and all major download sites. Philip is also a performance artist in his own right, and his highly charged readings of his ongoing poetry sequence *Lovesongs for Extinct Creatures* have proved increasingly popular in recent years. He has won both the *Evening Standard*'s Most Promising Newcomer to British Film and Most Promising Playwright Awards – the only person ever to receive both prizes.

MOYA PRODUCTIONS LTD

Aron Rollin recently formed Moya Productions in order to focus on bringing new writing to the London stage. He was previously a co-producer with SPL. Recent productions include the Fringe First winning *The Rap Guide to Evolution* which transferred to New York for an extended run this year and was subsequently turned into a series of short films. Aron also produced *The Rebel Cell* which won a prestigious *What's on Stage* award and enjoyed a successful London run and nationwide tour. Other works include Ariel Dorfman's *Speak Truth to Power* with Bill Night and Rufus Sewell and Clara Brennan's *Bud Take the Wheel.*

Caitlin Albery Beavan formed Moya Productions in collaboration with Aron and previously worked with him at SPL as a general manager. She has also independently produced *Elegy* (Shunt), The Bacchae (The Deaf Institute), *What Shall We Tell Caroline?* (The White Bear), *Talking In Bed* (Theatre503), *A Butcher Of Distinction* (Cock Tavern/King's Head). Caitlin is a co-founder of Theatre Ninjas and is a recent recipient of the Stage One Bursary for new theatre producers.

Moya Productions would like to give special thanks to all at the Southwark Playhouse and would also like to thank the following for their support:

David Charles, Adam Speers, Billie Temple, Stuart Allen, all at Out of Joint, Marc Connell, all at Methuen Drama, Andrew Weatherall, Jenny Beavan, Stephen Pidcock and Ben Chamberlain at The Corner Shop PR, Anoushka Warden, Emily Bevan and Matt Hatt of Masterclass, Danielle Tarento, Supporting Wall, Jessica Ronane and Fiona Kyle.

SOUTHWARK PLAYHOUSE

'Southwark Playhouse's brand is as quirky as it is classy'
The Stage

Southwark Playhouse Theatre Company was founded in 1993 by Juliet Alderdice, Tom Wilson and Mehmet Ergen. They identified the need for a high quality accessible theatre which would provide opportunities for the best emerging companies and practitioners, and also act as a major resource for the local community. They leased a disused workshop in a then comparatively neglected part of Southwark and turned it into a flexible theatre space.

The theatre quickly put down strong roots in Southwark, developing an innovative, free at source education programme. It has worked closely with teachers, Southwark Borough Council, businesses and government agencies to improve educational achievement and raise aspirations. This programme is in great demand and attracts substantial funding each year.

Over the past fifteen years the theatre has established itself as one of London's leading studio theatres, representing high quality work by new and emerging theatre practitioners.

In 2007 it moved to its current premises in vaults beneath Platform 1 of London Bridge Station where it is home to a 150-seat studio theatre and a brand new secondary performance space, The Vault, which now serves as a platform for developing and nurturing cutting edge theatre.

Under successive talented artistic directors, Mehmet Ergen (now Artistic Director of the Arcola Theatre), Erica Whyman (now Artistic Director of the Northern Stage Company), Thea Sharrock (recently directed *After the Dance* at the National Theatre and *Cause Célèbre* at the Old Vic), Gareth Machin (now Artistic Director of Salisbury Playhouse) and Ellie Jones, Southwark Playhouse has become an indispensable part of theatre in London.

2011 marked the start of Chris Smyrnios' tenure as Artistic Director and an exciting programme of work that included Philip Ridley's first world premiere in three years, *Tender Napalm*, major revivals of Stephen Sondheim's *Company* and Hannah Cowley's *The Belle's Stratagem* and the critically acclaimed *Parade* and *Bound*, both of which received five star reviews in the *Evening Standard*. The year culminated with Southwark Playhouse being the recipient of the Peter Brook Empty Space Award 2011 with Fiona Mountford praising the 'high-energy, life-giving spirit' of the theatre.

2012 is Southwark Playhouse's last year in its current home before it relocates to a temporary premise to make way for the redevelopment of London Bridge Station.

For more information about our forthcoming season and to book tickets visit **www.southwarkplayhouse.co.uk.** You can also support us online by joining our Facebook and Twitter pages.

Staff List

Patrons Sir Michael Caine, Peter Gill OBE, Simon Hughes MP, Andy Serkis

Artistic Director Chris Smyrnios
General Manager Alys Mayer
Press and Marketing Manager Susie Safavi
Technical Manager Richard Seary
Front of House and Bar Manager Mark Bromley
Schools Programme Manager Stewart Melton
Young Company Co-Ordinator Paul Edwards
Associate Director David Mercatali
Associate Producer Jethro Compton

Shivered

I can be happy in what you call the dark
but which, to me, is golden . . .
Hellen Keller

We plough the dust of stars
and drink the universe
in a glass of rain.
Ihab Hassan

. . . time is the fire in which we burn.
Delmore Schwartz

Characters

Alec
Ryan
Jack
Lyn
Gordy
Evie
Mikey

Note: scene numbering denotes the chronological order of events.

Act One

5

A hostage cell.

Alec, *twenties, hands tied.*

He is beaten, traumatised.

He goes to say something, then stops.

Eventually . . .

Alec Monsters . . .

Pause.

Monsters . . .

Pause.

Monsters . . .

12

Wasteground. Night.

Ryan *appears, carrying a bag, followed by* **Jack**.

They are both twelve and holding torches.

Jack *is limping,* **Ryan** *wears glasses.*

Jack Slow down.

Ryan Sorry – You need help?

Jack No. Just don't go sprinting ahead like some fucking . . . sprinting ahead fucker.

Ryan Watch out for the barbed wire.

Jack *What* barbed wire?

Ryan It sort of . . . springs up.

Jack Fucking hell.

Ryan Well, *you* wanted to come!

Jack I *do*. Just didn't realise we were – How far we fucking going?

Ryan The canal.

Jack Oh, do fuck off.

Ryan That's where the monster was seen.

Jack Coming *out* of the canal what's-his-name said.

Ryan Mr Chembow.

Jack 'I saw the creature coming out of the canal,' said Mr Chembow.

Ryan That's right.

Jack Well . . . here's 'out', ain't it?

Ryan A bit further.

Jack No, mate! My legs're fucking hurting. I can feel the veins knotting together like . . . like knotting together stuff. They hurt! Fuck!

Ryan Okay, okay, I guess this is close enough.

Jack A million miles back was close enough.

Ryan You can sit down if you like.

Jack There's broken glass and crap everywhere.

Ryan Not here there's not.

Jack Well, *you* sit down then.

Ryan I am.

Jack Go right ahead. Just don't come crying to me if a rusty nail punctures one of your bollocks.

Ryan *sits and opens his bag.*

Jack Fuck me, it's dark – What's that noise?

Ryan . . . Can't hear anything.

Jack Drug addicts shoot up in the old factory, you know. What if one of them goes ape-shit and wants to rape us.

Ryan I can't see anyone.

Jack They could be secretly watching. Having a wank to get in the mood.

Ryan Oh, do shut up.

Jack It's what they're like, mate. They watch . . . they get in the mood . . . Next thing you know, your arsehole looks like spaghetti with meat balls.

Ryan Go back if you're that scared.

Jack Who said anything about scared, for fuck's sake!? Jesus.

Ryan *has got a tripod from bag.*

Ryan Help me with this.

Jack What is it?

Ryan Tripod. This leg's a bit stiff – Pull!

Jack *pulls leg.*

Ryan Harder!

Tripod leg opens up.

Ryan Yesss!

Jack What's it for?

Ryan This.

Gets camera out of bag.

Jack Fuck me, that's some camera.

Ryan My dad's.

Starts attaching camera to tripod.

Jack Don't he mind you using it?

Ryan Dad . . . he's away on important business at the moment.

Jack You mean he's fucked off and left you.

Ryan . . . Sort of, yeah.

Jack Mine too. Never seen him.

Ryan Mine'll be back.

Jack Yeah, yeah, sure he will.

Ryan He fucking will.

Jack Okay, okay.

Indicates camera.

Has it got night vision stuff?

Ryan Not really. But the quality's still good.

Jack We don't want it all grainy. People never watch grainy clips.

Ryan It won't be too grainy. And it'll be nice and steady.

Jack Great. Wobbly clips cause blindness and, in some cases, brain tumours.

Ryan *has now attached camera to tripod.*

He looks through lens.

Ryan Okay . . . If anything comes out of the canal – We're ready!

Jack . . . So! What now?

Ryan We wait . . . I've got something to eat somewhere.

Looks in bag.

Oh! I did this.

Jack What?

Ryan A drawing. Of the monster.

Gives sheet of paper from bag to **Jack**.

Jack Fuck me! Look at those teeth.

Ryan I based them on a Tyrannosaurus Rex.

Jack I like the way you've done the skin.

Ryan The green scales took forever.

Jack Wish I could draw this good.

Ryan It's easy. I'll teach you if you like.

Jack Really?

Ryan Yeah.

Jack Oh, mate. Thank you – What's that?

Ryan . . . I can't hear anything.

Jack You sure?

Ryan Sure.

Slight pause.

Jack *sits.*

Jack They're discovering new creatures all the time, you know.

Ryan Yeah, I know.

Jack I did some research. They discovered a new kind of cow. It was up this mountain in Vietnam or somewhere. They called it the pseudo oryx – What's that noise?

Ryan . . . I didn't hear anything.

Slight pause.

Jack You heard about that creature in China?

Ryan What creature?

Jack The Hee-Qwa-Nyaa Monster. It lives in this river or lake or something. It's been seen by lots of people. They said it has big teeth and makes a noise like a strangled dolphin, whatever the fuck that's supposed to sound like. Someone filmed it. You can't see much cos it's at night but it's a big fucker. Elephant big. Two people went out to find it. They found their remains two weeks later. Mangled. The monster had eaten their heads and legs – What's that? Fuck!

Ryan You're scaring yourself.

Jack Mate, we're alone. It's night. There's something out there that just might want to eat us. That is not *me* scaring *me*. That's *everything else* fucking scaring me.

Ryan Jack! Relax. Okay?

Jack We need a fucking weapon or something.

Ryan All indications are the creature's more afraid of us than we are of it.

Jack You wanna fucking bet?

Ryan Look, what's more risky? Sitting here at night waiting for . . . whatever's in that canal. Or walking the streets during the day waiting to get beat up by Krafer and his fucking gang? Eh? You can barely walk cos that bastard's kicked you so fucking hard.

Slight pause.

Jack You're right, mate.

Ryan Okay.

Jack Okay . . . Did you say you had something to eat?

Ryan Oh . . . yeah.

Jack I'm fucking starving.

Ryan *gets food from bag.*

Ryan Sandwich?

Jack What's in it?

Ryan Marmite and baked beans.

Jack Great!

They eat.

Ryan Why's Krafer picking on you all the time?

Jack Fuck knows. He picks on my mum too. Follows her down the street calling her 'weirdo' and 'fat'. A few weeks ago he said he wanted to slice off her tits to make parachutes. She's afraid to leave the fucking house now.

Ryan Ain't she told the police?

Jack Hundreds of fucking times. They do fuck all. One time Krafer and his gang locked me in a shed. They said they were gonna set fire to it. I could smell the petrol and everything. I heard them striking matches. I screamed so much I lost my voice. Someone must've heard. No one did a fucking thing. I tell you, mate, if I'm ever found dead – beaten up sort of thing – promise me you'll tell the police who did it. Big Prick Krafer and his gang of fucking . . . whatever.

Ryan That won't happen, Jack.

Jack But you *promise*, Ryan?

Ryan Yeah, mate, of course – You hear that?

Jack What?

Ryan Shhh! Listen!

Jack Oh, Jesus.

Ryan . . . It's coming from the canal.

Jack I was afraid it was.

Ryan *turns off torch.*

Ryan Turn your torch off.

Jack Are you fucking kidding?

Ryan Off.

Jack Fuck.

Turns torch off.

Ryan *turns camera on.*

Jack Is it recording?

Ryan Yeah.

Jack . . . See anything?

Ryan . . . *Something's* out there.

Jack Oh, shit.

Ryan It's getting closer.

Jack Fuck . . .

Ryan Shhh.

Slight pause.

Jack *is whimpering.*

Jack It's gonna eat us . . . I know it is . . .

Ryan Closer . . .

Jack*'s whimpering gets louder and louder.*

Jack It's gonna eat us . . .

Ryan I see it!

Jack *screams.*

14

Office in derelict factory. Day.

Lyn*, forties, has her hands tied.*

Gordy, *twenties, is holding a lit cigarette.*

Gordy Scream. Go on. No one'll hear you. No one that gives a fuck anyway.

Lyn Please . . . I don't know anything.

Gordy I know you don't.

Lyn Then why?

Gordy It's fun.

Lyn *spits in* **Gordy***'s face.*

Gordy *goes to punch her, then stops.*

Gordy Oh, no, no. I'm not going to spoil that pretty face of yours. Not yet. I want to enjoy it first. You know what I'm going to do? I'm going to ram my cock between your lips. Then I'm going to force it all the way down your throat till you gag and –

Lyn Oww.

Gordy What?

Lyn Cramp.

Gordy Where?

Lyn Leg – Oww!

Gordy Which one?

Lyn Left.

Gordy *rubs her leg.*

Lyn Lower.

Gordy Here?

Lyn Yeah – Oh, Jesus! . . . Well, *rub* it, then, *rub* it!

Gordy I am.

Lyn You're not. You're *squeezing* it – Oh, I'll do it.

Shakes ropes from her hands.

Gordy I was just getting into it then, you know.

Lyn You're getting a bit bloody close with that cigarette.

Gordy Sorry.

Lyn *is rubbing leg.*

Slight pause.

Gordy What did you say your job was?

Lyn Eh?

Gordy When you used to work here?

Lyn Oh. Canteen.

Gordy Can't see you doing that somehow.

Lyn Really?

Gordy Yeah. A woman like you –

Lyn (*overlapping*) 'A woman like me'?

Gordy – something more . . . managerial.

Lyn I told you. No flattery.

Gordy It's true. I can see you sitting here. In this office. Cool. In control.

Slight pause.

Where was it? The canteen.

Lyn Ground floor.

Gordy Must've been busy – Factory this size.

Lyn Five thousand dinners on an average day.

Gordy Fuck me, you must've been knackered.

Lyn Well, I didn't cook them single-handed.

Slight pause.

Gordy Make a good hotel, I reckon. This place.

Lyn Oh, give me a break.

Gordy It *would*. Turn all these old offices into rooms. How many are there?

Lyn I don't know. Lots.

Gordy And that big open space in the main factory. Room for an indoor swimming pool there. Solarium. That canal out back – little bit of landscaping, it could look like Venice. Put a few of those banana-shaped boats on it – what they called?

Lyn Gondolas.

Gordy That's the ones! Tables and chairs by the water's edge. Ice cream. Sexy tenors in stripy shirts. I could be one of those. I'm great at karaoke. I won a competition when I was sixteen, you know. Oh, yeah. Slap-up dinner for two at a *Venus Steak House*. Took that make-up artist I was telling you about. She said the only way to eat steak was rare. My plate turned up full of blood. Soaked into my boiled potatoes. Made them look like beetroots. Couldn't eat a fucking thing. I'd ban rare steak in my hotel. Doner kebabs. Make them our speciality. Give the hotel a theme.

Lyn Doner kebabs and gondolas?

Gordy Yeah!

Lyn *shakes her head.*

Gordy Why not?

Lyn 'Why not'? You mean, apart from it being the most ridiculous idea I've ever heard?

Gordy I don't think it's a ridicul –

Lyn This place was meant to be a car plant. You understand that? A place where people could work. Earn a living. Have their self-respect. Look after their families – Responsibility. Duty. Things a man like you wouldn't know anything about.

Slight pause.

What's that?

Gordy Eh?

Lyn I . . . I heard something.

Gordy No . . .

Lyn Shhh! . . . Corridor.

Gordy Wouldn't your son let us know if anyone had –

Lyn My son's not here.

Gordy Well, he was keeping watch the other times.

Lyn Well, he's *not* keeping watch *this* time – Are you going to check outside or shall I do it?

Gordy *goes outside.*

Slight pause.

Lyn *gets mobile and dials.*

Lyn (*into mobile*) Hello, Ryan, love . . . How are you feeling? . . . Well, you just stay in bed and rest. Mum'll get you a little present on the way home. Some comics. Would you like some comics? . . . What ones?

Gordy *returns.*

Lyn*'s back is to him.*

Lyn Ryan, Mum's very sorry she left you today . . . You're right – Mum should have stayed at home when you're not feeling well and . . . she's very sorry . . . she's very sorry . . . I love you too.

Hangs up.

Slight pause.

Turns to see **Gordy**.

Gordy Nothing.

Indicates the corridor.

Lyn . . . Tie me up again.

Gordy Sure?

Lyn Why wouldn't I be?

Gordy All-right!

Ties her hands and feet.

Lyn Gently. I'm not a piece of fairground rigging.

Gordy . . . Ready?

Lyn . . . Yes.

Slight pause.

Gordy I'm gonna force my cock down your throat and fuck your face and –

Lyn Shhh!

Gordy Oh, not again.

Lyn I'm not imagining it. I heard . . . I did . . . I did . . .

Struggles with ropes.

Untie me. What have you . . . ? Untie me! Untie –

Gordy Alright, alright, calm down.

Unties her.

Lyn *rushes outside.*

Lyn (*shouting, off*) Hello? . . . Hello?

Pause.

Lyn *returns.*

Lyn There was . . . something . . .

Gordy Probably a fox. I saw a big one while I was waiting for you. They're so tame now. It came right up to me.

Lyn . . . Give me a cigarette please.

Gordy *gives her cigarette and lights it.*

Gordy Are you . . . okay?

Lyn Yes. I'm fine.

Slight pause.

Gordy Lyn . . . I know what . . . happened.

Lyn . . . Oh?

Gordy To your eldest son.

Lyn . . . Who told you?

Gordy Someone saw us talking. At the fair.

Lyn Of *course* they did. 'Know what happened to her? Her son was killed. Wanna know how? It was horrible. Wanna know all the gruesome details?'

Gordy It wasn't like that.

Lyn Wasn't it?

Gordy No. They said what you'd been through was hell.

Lyn Hell? That all? – It was Cheryl, wasn't it?

Gordy Cheryl?

Lyn Who told you. Green coat.

Gordy Yeah.

Lyn I saw her. By the Big Wheel. We used to be neighbours.

Gordy She said, yeah.

Lyn Well, I hope she told you what she said to me. 'Oh, I know how you feel. I remember when I lost my baby.' 'Your *baby*?' I said. 'You're comparing a cot death to what happened to my son. My Alec was twenty-four years old. Not twenty bloody months! I've had twenty years of worrying about him, measles, two sprained ankles, athletic competitions, watching him learn to read, write, drive, twenty Christmases, twenty birthdays. For twenty-four years my Alec was . . . Alec was . . .'

Slight pause.

Gordy Cheryl . . . she said your son's a hero. There's plans for a statue. War memorial. That must make you proud.

Pause.

Cheryl said –

Lyn Jesus! Is there anything she *didn't* tell you? My whole life story laid out like . . . like the stations of the bloody cross – Let me guess. My husband's gone missing.

Gordy . . . Yeah.

Lyn Well, don't you worry about that. He'll be back.

Gordy How d'you know?

Lyn Because it's what he does. Mikey. When his dad died – know what Mikey did? Packed a bag and – whoosh! Vanished! I had a three-year-old son. Living on a gang-ridden estate in Hackney. I would've been worried sick if I wasn't so busy putting food on the table. Then guess who strolls back? Casual as you like.

Slight pause.

Gordy I want to help you, Lyn.

Lyn *does not respond.*

Gordy I want to . . . to . . .

Lyn To? To? To?

Slowly, **Gordy** *goes to* **Lyn**.

He starts to embrace her.

Lyn *does not respond.*

Gordy *continues.*

Suddenly, **Lyn** *makes the decision to kiss him.*

She does so with surprising ferocity.

Gordy *kisses her back.*

Lyn *gets ever more passionate.*

Then, as suddenly as she started, she stops.

She struggles to get away from **Gordy**.

Lyn No. I'm married – Stop, Gordy! No!

Pushes herself away.

Gordy Jesus! Lyn.

Lyn I'm not this! I'm not!

Gordy Then why are we bloody here? Eh? This is the third time and all we do is . . . *what* are we doing? Tell me!

Pause.

Lyn We organised a welcome-home party – the last time Alec was on leave. Ryan was in charge of the music. Some friends from church popped round. I was in the kitchen with them when I heard Alec's voice. Shouting. Angry. I rushed to the living room. Alec was jabbing his finger at Ravi – Cheryl's husband. Accusing him of picking up young girls and turning them into prostitutes. Everyone was very still. The music stopped. It was like one of those moments in a film – what's it called? Freeze frame. Then suddenly Alec's mood changed. 'Where's the music? Dance, everyone! Dance!'

Slight pause.

The next day was a Sunday. I cooked a roast chicken. Alec's favourite. We were halfway through the meal when he turned on *me*. He accused me of . . . things I can't even bring myself to . . .

Gordy He didn't mean it, Lyn.

Lyn Please don't say anything, Gordy, because I tell you, in all honesty, there is not one word you can utter on this subject that will not make me hate you.

Slight pause.

My son had become a bomb. We had to constantly de-fuse him. We were never sure what would set him off. One day, Mikey was watching athletics on telly. He said one of the runners was 'going great guns'. 'What's great about guns, Dad? You ever been shot at?' Poor Mikey. He was afraid to open his mouth.

Slight pause.

We had one good day. I asked Alec not to go back. *Begged* him. I didn't care what the repercussions were. Alec agreed. No argument, no struggle. He just let me hold him . . . I phoned my sister in Australia. I said my prayers have been answered. But the next day Alec changed his mind. He asked an old school friend – Dermot something or other – to take him to the station. He wouldn't let me kiss him goodbye. As he got into the car he looked at me and – oh, God, that look! Did he see something in me I'd never –

A mobile rings.

Lyn Wh-what's that?

Gordy It's a phone.

Lyn Yours?

Gordy No.

Searches office.

Lyn Where's it coming from?

Gordy Shhh!

Continues to search.

Lifts some sheets of hardboard etc.

Gordy Oh, fuck!

Lyn What?

Gordy It's a kid.

Lyn No.

Gordy He's hurt bad.

Lyn Oh, God.

Gordy Don't look!

Lyn Is he alive?

Gordy . . . Barely.

Lyn God. God.

Gets her mobile.

Gordy No! I'll call.

Gets his mobile and dials.

Don't get involved.

Lyn But I –

Gordy No! Us. Here. Questions will be asked – (*into mobile*) Ambulance!

Lyn *is hesitating.*

Gordy You've got a son, Lyn – Go!

Lyn . . . Don't leave him.

Gordy I won't – (*Into mobile.*) Hello, I'm at the old Draylingstowe car plant. There's a boy. He's unconscious and . . . Eh? Drugs? I don't think so. There's blood.

Lyn *rushes out.*

11

Living room. Day.

Evie, *thirties, is in armchair.*

Evie (*into mobile*) Hello, Barbra, how are you, honey? . . . I know, I know, it's about this time it starts hitting home, love, when all the rushing about's over – the funeral stuff, which is draining beyond belief, not to mention the expense, which we won't go into, cos we'll pay anything for loved ones, wouldn't we, hon, and do they know it, don't go there, we won't – You don't mind me calling, do you, love? . . . Sure? Cos if you do just tell me to stop sticking my silly ol' nose in and I'll hang up this instant, I swear I will, and I won't feel the least bit offended, you know me, skin as thick as a rhinoceros, face like one too according to my son – ha, ha . . .

Well, you've got to laugh, Barbra, in the face of life's slings and whatsits, that's what my old dad used to say, bless him, even when he'd lost both legs to sugar and couldn't see a sausage unless it was lit up like a Christmas tree – What, love? . . . Now, let's have no more of that talk, Barbra! D'you think your Jonny would've wanted you saying such things? . . . Course not. He would've wanted you to get on with your life and be happy. Didn't he say as much to you before he passed over? . . . Course he did. 'You're still a good-looking woman.' That's what he said? Am I right? . . . Well, I told you I'd call if he made contact, didn't I? . . . Last night, love. Fast asleep I was when all of a sudden – I jolt awake and there was your Jonny. Standing by the window. His hair's all thick and curly like it was before the chemo – oh, shush, hon, no tears, no tears. Jonny said, 'Tell my Barbra she's got to –' Oh, love, my phone's gonna run out of power any second. Can I book you for session perhaps and I can tell you everything. Do you want a half hour or an hour?

Jack *comes in.*

Evie An hour works out cheaper and my little Jack will keep us well watered with cups of tea – Won't you, love?

Jack Yes, Mum.

Evie Bless him . . . No, no, cash only, love, if that's okay – Wh-what's going on? Hello, hello? . . . Wh-who's this? . . . Oh, hello, Kieran, I was just talking to your mum, love, is something wrong? . . . Me? . . . Oh, Kieran, how can you say such things, I'm trying to *help* your mum, for goodness' sake . . . Oh, I can hear your poor mum crying in the background, please put her back on, love, you're grieving and it makes us do and say things we don't really – He's hung up!

Jack He'll phone back.

Evie I was trying to help, wasn't I?

Jack Some people don't want help.

Evie His poor mother does. I'll be haunted by the sound of her crying all night – Oh, I'm gonna call back right now, hon, I really am!

Jack Later, Mum.

Evie You think?

Jack Tell me her address. I'll go round there. Say hello as she goes out shopping.

Evie Book her in for an hour.

Jack Two if you like.

Evie Two's best. She needs a lot of comforting.

Jack Another drink?

Indicates empty glass near **Evie**.

Evie Just a small one.

Jack *takes glass.*

Evie You're an angel, Jack. Really you are. So wise. You must be the reincarnation of someone like Gandhi. I've always said it. Haven't I? Eh? – You got my ciggies?

Jack Ciggies?

Evie I left two messages . . . Oh, don't tell me you've lost another phone.

Jack Krafer and his mates stole it again.

Hands drink to **Evie**.

Evie You've got to stay out of their way, hon.

Jack I try. But they won't stay out of mine.

Mobile rings.

Evie *answers it.*

Evie Barbra, love, is everything okay? . . . No, no, I understand . . . The poor boy's lost his dad. Grief *is* like a kind of madness – Oh, love! My battery! Quick! Shall I book you in tomorrow? Three o'clock? How about a two-hour session? I think we need it – Perfect!

Hangs up.

Jack Yesss!

Evie I will sleep easy tonight.

Downs drink.

One more!

Holds out empty glass.

Jack Coming right up!

Takes glass and pours drink.

Evie And don't drown it with the orange juice, hon. You know my knees start to grind together if there's not enough alcohol in my blood.

Jack Try that.

Gives drink to **Evie**.

Evie Jack . . . you're standing a bit funny.

Jack Krafer kicked me, didn't he.

Evie Oh, that boy doesn't know his own strength.

Jack It hurts when I breathe deep.

Evie Perhaps you've got a broken rib.

Jack You think?

Evie Let me see.

Lifts **Jack**'*s shirt.*

Oh, Jack . . .

Sees bruise on his back.

Jack What?

Evie There's a big bruise – Hang on! Where's my pen?

Picks up a felt-tip pen.

Jack What you doing?

Evie Keep still.

Starts drawing on bruise.

Jack Oww! It hurts, Mum.

Evie Still! . . . There!

Picks up mobile.

We need a photo of that.

Takes photo.

Jack Of what?

Evie One more.

Takes photo.

Jack Mum!

Evie Jack, hon. Look at me. Look!

Jack *turns to face* **Evie**.

Evie The bruise on your back. It's the face of Jesus.

16

Community hall. Night.

Gordy *is speaking into a microphone.*

He is full of evangelist energy and fervour.

Gordy Ladies and gentlemen, I have a story to tell. It is a sad story, a shocking story and, in places, yes, I warn you now, a horrific story. It is the story of a man we will call . . . G.

Slight pause.

Imagine this . . . A run-down flat on a run-down estate. Damp. Rats. Graffiti. It is here our Baby G was born to a mother who was little more than a child herself. Is it any wonder this poor mother found it difficult to cope? Is it any wonder she put some vegetables on the gas cooker to boil and then left the kitchen, leaving two-year-old little Baby G playing under the kitchen table? – Oh, ladies and gentlemen, be warned, what I'm about to tell you is distressing in the extreme! Baby G sees magical mist coming from the saucepan. Baby G reaches up and – Oh, the screams! Baby G is scarred for life! His face. His chest. His . . . his poor little genitals – I know, I know, it's stressful to hear such terrible things but you have to know in order to understand what poor Baby G's life was like after this tragic accident. Children pointing and laughing. Going into a shop and having the shopkeeper say, 'Why, that's the most horrific mask I've ever seen.' And, as you grow into a teenager, no girl wanting to go out with you, let alone touch you, kiss you. And there's worse to come, ladies and gentlemen! Your mother casts you out like something vile and unclean. Is it any wonder this scarred wreck of a human being ends up taking drugs to find escape from his hell? But the brief euphoria of illegal drugs is no answer. *You* know that. *I* know that. And in his heart – his big and yearning to be loved heart – our nineteen-year-old – one time Baby G, now Mr G – he knew this too. Ladies and gentlemen, I have a photograph to show you. It is a photograph of our Mr G. I should warn you, it is not an easy photograph to look at. Women in the audience, and those of a nervous disposition, might want to avert their eyes.

Reveals photo.

Look at it and weep – Madam, are you okay? . . . We need first aid here! First aid! . . . Look at his poor scarred, teenaged face! Look at his scarred chest! His hair all scalded away. You notice the way the tightening of the damaged skin has hunched him over, made it impossible for him to walk upright . . . Oh, it breaks my heart to see it!

Conceals photo.

Imagine this: that poor creature – he decides his life was not worth living! Yes, ladies and gentlemen, Mr G decides to kill himself! He goes to the old Draylingstowe car plant. He finds a length of electrical wire – yes, *wire*, ladies and gentlemen! He ties one end of the wire round his neck. He stands on a chair. He ties the other end of the wire to a pipe in the ceiling. He is just about to kick the chair from under him when . . . A noise! A tiny whimper! It sounds like . . . Yes! A child! Where's it coming from? Mr G takes the wire from his neck and jumps off the chair. There it is again! But where? Mr G starts frantically searching amongst the rubble. He throws things aside. And then he lifts some rubble and – A boy! Oh, the boy is injured and covered with blood. Mr G kneels beside him. The boy is unconscious. 'Don't worry! I'll get help' – And then the child grabs Mr G's finger. And it's like an electric current goes from the boy into Mr G. And Mr G – he feels all the poisons in his blood cleanse away. And more! Mr G feels his scarred skin become supple and smooth once more. Joints start to move with a freedom he hasn't known since he was a child. His back straightens. Hair grows back. And when he stands . . . it's as if all the horrors and cruelty of Mr G's life have never been. Mr G stands straight. Mr G stands proud. Mr G knows he has a future. And how do I know all this? Because *I* am Mr G! Yes! Look how I have been healed! Look! Look!

Removes shirt.

Not a scar! Not a blemish! I will come down into the audience soon and let you feel just how free from scars my body is! You can feel for yourselves how smooth my skin is.

Slight pause.

The Blessed Jack! That was the boy who healed me! He survived his injuries, ladies and gentlemen. The Blessed Jack survived one of the most vicious beatings ever known and he rose from that rubble to become the healing prophet he now is. Some of you, I know, have seen evidence of his miracles in film clips and photographs but now, here, tonight, you can meet him in person. Ladies and gentlemen, I present to you Draylingstowe's very own miracle-worker – the Blessed Jack!

Claps.

Nothing happens.

Slight pause.

The Blessed Jack!

Nothing happens.

One moment, ladies and gentlemen.

Walks off.

Heated words between **Gordy** *and* **Evie** *are heard off.*

Gordy *returns with* **Jack**.

Jack *is in a wheelchair, seriously brain damaged.*

Gordy Ladies and gentlemen, please forgive that little delay there. Jack's mother was supposed to bring her Blessed Jack out to meet you but . . . oh, she has not been out in public like this for many, many years. Some of you know her – The Miraculous Evie . . . Yes, yes, I see many faces radiate affection and love for her – Miraculous Evie has been of great help to the wonderful Barbra, who's here with us tonight, and who helped get this old community centre up and running again for this meeting. She's here with her wonderful son, Kieran – Mate, I know you have had your doubts about the Miraculous Evie and Blessed Jack but . . . well, I hope, after tonight, all those doubts will come to an end – What's that, Blessed Jack?

Leans close to **Jack**.

Gordy Mmm . . . yes, of course – The Blessed Jack wants you to know his healing is not bound to any specific creed or religion. All the magical healing powers of the universe find a channel through our Blessed Jack. It matters not what your faith – Christian, Muslim, Jew, Hindu, Sikh, Humanist, Atheist, Communist, Capitalist – all are welcome. In short, all can be healed – What's that, Blessed Jack?

Leans close to **Jack**.

Gordy There's someone here tonight with a sugar diabetic problem . . . Is there such a person? . . . You, madam! Jack wants to heal you! . . . What, Jack?

Leans close to **Jack**.

Gordy Someone with a cancerous growth! Jack will heal you! . . . Angina! Herpes! Arthritis! Cystitis! Leukaemia! Bulimia! Chlamydia! Obesity! Infertility! Coma! Melanoma! Depression! Whatever the problem, whatever the cause, from bad breath to menopause – Be healed! Be healed! Be healed!

10

Wasteground at back of factory. Day.

Ryan *is searching the rubble.*

Slight pause.

Jack *rushes on –*

Jack Fuck! You scared me.

Ryan . . . Sorry.

Jack I ain't here. Okay?

Ryan . . . Okay.

Jack *hides.*

Ryan *carries on searching.*

Pause.

Jack Can you see Krafer and his mates?

Ryan I don't know who Krafer and his mates are.

Jack You're lucky . . . Can you see any kids hanging round at all?

Ryan . . . No.

Jack You sure?

Ryan Yeah.

Jack *comes out of hiding.*

Jack They got me down by the roundabout, didn't they. My phone – that's gone. Second one this month. Mum'll have a fucking fit. Jesus – Aww! They've kicked my legs to shit again.

Ryan You should sit down.

Jack Can't do that, mate. If I stop moving my blood could turn thick as custard – Don't let me disturb you, mate. Ignore me.

Paces around, wincing.

What's your name?

Ryan Ryan.

Jack I'm Jack.

Slight pause.

You here by yourself?

Ryan My mum's in there somewhere.

Jack In the old factory?

Ryan Yeah.

Jack Drugs?

Ryan No.

Jack Prostitute?

Ryan No.

Jack But she's with a man, right?

Ryan . . . Yeah.

Jack You out here keeping guard or something?

Ryan . . . Yeah.

Jack Fuck me. Can't she go to a hotel? Be a bit more comfortable than an old fucking car plant. Unless old car plants turn her on.

Ryan It's not that.

Jack Nothing to be ashamed of, mate. People get turned on by all sorts of things – Firemen! Women like firemen. Men – they like nurses. Enemas. You seen any clips of men getting enemas?

Ryan No.

Jack There's this one – A man dresses up like a pig. He's on all fours. Then this nurse shoves a tube up his arse and pours like a million pints of Guinness into him. The man's going 'oink-oink' 'n' stuff. You know? Then he sort of crawls around. The nurse is saying, 'Hold it in, you dirty piggy-wiggy.' But then there's this massive 'Oink!' from the man and all the Guinness comes squirting out his arsehole – Whooosh!

Ryan Really.

Jack Yeah. So all I'm saying is . . . compared to what some people get off on, your mum being kinky about car plants ain't nothing.

Ryan Mum ain't kinky about car plants.

Jack Why ain't she doing it – whatever her 'it' is – somewhere else then?

Ryan Because she don't fucking want to. Okay?

Jack Okay, okay. Jesus.

Slight pause.

Jack Hang on! . . . I know who you are! You were in the local paper. Your family.

Ryan My brother's head was cut off.

Jack Fuck! I *knew* it. I've seen the clip and everything.

Ryan Yeah.

Jack Alec Tyler! That's your brother's name, right?

Ryan Yeah.

Jack That is one famous clip, mate. *Everyone's* seen it.

Ryan I haven't.

Jack Why not?

Ryan He was my fucking brother.

Jack Okay, okay . . . Fuck! I am actually talking to Alec Tyler's brother.

Ryan Yeah.

Jack There was this girl. Gemma Burns. She's the year above me. She said she thought watching something like that was disgusting. She don't watch anything. Not even bullfights or dogs being sick. She's a right stuck-up cunt. I don't like her. Don't know anyone who does. Three kids held her down in the toilets and made her watch your brother. They had it on a mobile. They held it right up to her eyes. If she closed her eyes they hit her. Gemma was screaming and crying. She threw up over this kid's trainers when she saw all your brother's blood and everything. Everyone laughed. I wasn't there but I've seen the film of it. Teachers said we ain't supposed to watch it but everyone has. Gemma Burns's mum and dad took her out of school. They threatened to get the police in but nothing seemed to happen. Reece Jackson said they should break into Gemma's bedroom one night and hold her down like they did in the toilets, only *this* time make her watch the film of her throwing up while watching your brother's head being cut off. I said, if they did that, I'd like to be the one to film it.

Slight pause.

I think it's a fake anyway.

Ryan What?

Jack Your brother.

Ryan It's not.

Jack You ain't seen it, how d'you fucking know?

Ryan Cos my brother's fucking dead.

Jack He might be fucking dead, mate, but I tell you, that clip is none too convincing. The camera's wobbling way beyond the call of fucking duty. Always suspect if you want my opinion.

Ryan Which I don't.

Jack No need to be rude, mate. And your brother's screams?! Total shite. Like something out of a fucking horror film. Real screams ain't like that. Real screams're more . . . sort of – You seen the thing where the guy in the yellow shirt gets eaten by a bear.

Ryan No.

Jack AHHHHH! That's him. AHHHHH! But your brother – he's all sort of 'Oh, please, nooo. Please . . . NOOOO!' And his body – it don't even fucking jerk when the blade goes in. It's like nothing's happened. You seen that thing where the kid chewing gum gets half his hand cut off with a chainsaw.

Ryan No.

Jack Fuck, does he jump! Like a scorpion's just stung the tip of his fucking cock. You know? But your brother – he looks far too relaxed about the whole situation. Like he knows there's an ice-cold Fanta and a bag of peanuts waiting for him in the next room – I'm not pissing you off, am I?

Ryan Yes.

Jack Nearly finished. Your brother just don't *bleed* enough, mate. You seen that one where the woman's kid gets its head blown off on the beach.

Ryan No.

Jack Blood fountain. Everywhere. And that's just a toddler. Your brother he was – how old?

Ryan Twenty-four.

Jack I rest my case.

Slight pause.

Ryan They found Alec's head.

Jack Eh?

Ryan When they found his body.

Jack Where did they find it?

Ryan By a roadside somewhere.

Jack Is there film of it being found?

Ryan Film?

Jack Yeah, yeah. Something to actually *watch*.

Ryan I . . . I don't think so.

Jack How d'you know it happened, then?

Ryan Because . . . they told us.

Jack Who?

Ryan The men who came round. Soldiers. One was a general or something. We got a letter from the Prime Minister.

Jack You get the body back?

Ryan Yeah.

Jack Body *and* head.

Ryan Yeah.

Jack And the head was definitely not attached to the body?

Ryan No one said anything different.

Jack Well, I tell you this . . . if it wasn't a fucking fake – if it *wasn't* – then the Oscar for the most pathetic fucking beheading clip ever goes to . . . Alec Tyler.

Slight pause.

Jack Who's your mum having sex with?

Ryan Someone she met at the fair.

Jack Don't tell me. On the rollercoaster.

Ryan The fair ain't got a rollercoaster.

Jack Rollercoasters are a real turn-on for women. They like jerking their boyfriends off on them. You should check out rollercoastersuperspunkers dot com. The trick is to build the boyfriend up as the rollercoaster goes up. Then time it so as the rollercoaster plunges down – Whooosh! – the boyfriend cums. The orgasms're supposed to be out of this world. Mind you, spare a thought for the poor fuckers sitting behind, eh? 'What's that in my eye?' Ha!

Ryan *continues searching rubble.*

Jack What you lost?

Ryan Nothing. I'm looking for evidence.

Jack Of what?

Ryan You won't believe me.

Jack Try me.

Ryan Extra-terrestrial activity.

Jack Fuck me! . . . What's that?

Ryan Aliens.

Jack Outer space?

Ryan Yeah.

Jack Fuck me! And . . . what? You think aliens have been here.

Ryan I *know* they have.

Jack How?

Slight pause.

Come on, Ryan. You can tell me, mate.

Ryan Can I trust you, Jack?

Jack With your fucking life, mate.

Slight pause.

Ryan . . . It starts with a photograph.

Jack Of an alien!?

Ryan A UFO. The photograph was taken . . . from that hill. Over there!

Points.

Jack Motorway Mound.

Ryan Yeah. Years ago my mum and dad and brother went up there to take a family photograph. Mum was pregnant with me at the time. It was a hot day. The hottest day of the year. When they looked at the photograph later Dad noticed a light in the sky behind them. It was a flying saucer hovering –

Points above.

There.

Jack Above the car plant?!

Ryan Yeah.

Jack Fuck!

Ryan Dad took the photo to the local newspaper. They printed it. Lots of people wrote in saying Dad was being stupid and the light in the sky was clearly caused by the flash on the camera accidentally going off or something like that.

Jack That sounds like a load of bollocks to me.

Ryan Me too. And to Dad. So Dad carried on looking for UFOs.

Jack And?

Ryan He saw lots.

Jack Fuck!

Ryan There's more.

Jack Fuck!

Ryan After the car plant closed down Dad started this campaign called J.D.C.

Jack J.D.C.? I've heard of that.

Ryan *Justice for the Draylingstowe Children.*

Jack That's it.

Ryan Remember what it was for?

Jack Er . . . no.

Ryan My dad – he thought some of the paint the car company used caused children to be born with stuff like . . .

Holds out his hands.

This!

Jack Fuck!

Ryan You should've seen them before my operations.

Jack Fuck. So dodgy paint gave you . . . the hands of a mutant.

Ryan It's what Dad thought. But it wasn't.

Jack It wasn't?

Ryan No. You see, Dad had all the clues but he didn't make the right connections. That's why the court case against the car company collapsed. Dad made the mistake of seeing . . . illusory contours.

Jack What's that?

Ryan You mean you don't know what 'illusory contours' is?

Jack Er . . . no.

Ryan It's when you see shapes and connections where there ain't any. Like when you look at the stars at night and see the Plough or Pegasus.

Jack What're they?

Ryan Star constellations.

Jack Oh . . . okay, okay.

Ryan What I'm saying is . . . My dad – he had the information about UFOs. He had what happened to my hands and he had . . . This.

Takes newspaper clipping from pocket.

I only found it in my dad's things a few days ago.

Jack What is it?

Ryan Read it.

Jack I . . . I can't.

Ryan It's a newspaper article called 'The Monster of Draylingstowe Canal'.

Jack That canal?

Points.

Ryan Yeah. One of the security guards who worked at the car plant said he saw a strange creature. Three times. Always at night. Mr Chembow – that's the security guard's name –

he said, 'I saw it coming out of the canal.' He describes it as being the size of a car.

Jack Fuck!

Ryan It's got skin like a snake and teeth the size of carving knives.

Jack Fuck!

Ryan Mr Chembow took a photo – See?

Jack Where's the monster?

Ryan That shape in the water.

Jack . . . Fuck.

Ryan So . . . The monster. My mutant hands. They weren't caused by paint as Dad thought. Oh, no. They were caused by . . .

Looks up.

Alien contamination.

Jack *looks up.*

Jack Fucking fuck.

Ryan Yeah.

Jack You know what we should do? Come back here. At night. Get a clip of the monster coming out of the canal.

Ryan Yeah.

Jack A real fuck-off, total proof clip.

Ryan Yeah.

Jack All its teeth flashing.

Ryan Its scaly skin.

Jack And its roar – I wonder what it sounds like.

Ryan and **Jack** RAAAAAHHHH!!!

They laugh.

Jack . . . Mate, mate, you know what this could make us?

Ryan What?

Jack The stars of *YouTube*.

9

The fair. Day.

Lyn *is standing alone.*

Slight pause.

Gordy, *mid-twenties, approaches.*

Gordy Well, what have we here? The most beautiful woman at the fair.

Slight pause.

Know what seeing you here is like? Like seeing a unicorn in a muddy field full of donkeys. Anyone ever said that to you before?

Lyn Yes.

Slight pause.

Gordy That your son getting on the *Rocket to Mars*?

Lyn . . . Yes.

Gordy You can see for miles when it reaches the top.

Lyn What are you? Salesman? Pervert? Religious nut?

Gordy You are one suspicious lady.

Lyn (*calling to* **Ryan**) Go on, then! Get on!

Gordy He wants you to get on with him.

Lyn I know what he wants – (*Calling*.) I'll wait here! Go! Go!

Gordy Don't you want to take a rocket to Mars?

Lyn I've been. It's over-rated.

Gordy Look at your son. All that excitement on his face. We all need a bit of excitement. And what can be more exciting than – A raffle ticket!

Lyn Salesman.

Gordy First prize is a state-of-the-art, high-quality, hot-off-the-press camcorder perfect for capturing all those precious family moments – Oh, look at your boy as he gets in the rocket. Don't you wanna remember that all your life? Come on. Special offer. Ten tickets for the price of five.

Lyn . . . That smile of yours usually works, does it?

Gordy Usually, yeah.

Slight pause.

Lyn I'll take twenty.

Gordy Okay!

Lyn No. Thirty.

Gordy Well . . .

Lyn No, make that forty. No! Make it a round fifty. Why not? That means I get a hundred, right? A hundred chances to win first prize. No! I'll buy the lot! Come on! I've just got to have a camcorder for my precious family moments. How much money do you want?

Gordy Okay, stop it, stop.

Lyn Do you accept credit cards?

Gordy It's a scam. Okay? No one wins.

Lyn Oh, you *do* surprise me!

Slight pause.

Gordy Your son's waving at you.

Lyn I can see that.

Gordy *waves.*

Lyn What you doing?

Gordy I'm just trying to –

Lyn Well, don't – Haven't you got some candyfloss needs making or something?

Gordy I work on *The Twirling Tea Cups*.

Lyn *The Twirling Tea Cups*?

Gordy Don't say it like that.

Lyn Like what?

Gordy Like it's one step from mopping a mortuary.

Lyn I'm sure it's a very rewarding job.

Gordy It can be. When I'm on *The Cups* there's not a girl anywhere can resist grabbing hold of my tea spoon, if you get my drift. Especially if I've got my shirt off.

Lyn . . . Fancy yourself, don't you.

Gordy Not as much as you do.

Lyn How old are you?

Gordy How old d'you want me to be?

Slight pause.

How old are you?

Lyn . . . Forty-two.

Gordy Fuck! . . . Sorry, sorry, I just meant –

Lyn I *know* what you 'just meant'.

Gordy No, no, I mean . . . your kid! He's only – what? Ten?

Lyn Twelve.

Gordy Most women with kids that age? Early thirties. That's what you look like. Thirty-two tops.

Lyn Oh, don't start the flattery thing again.

Gordy I'm not. You look young for your age.

Lyn I do *not* look young for my age. I don't *want* to look young for my age.

Ryan *walks up.*

Ryan I feel sick.

Gordy Good view, though, yeah?

Ryan It stinks of petrol.

Gordy The engine was leaking yesterday – It's safe now! Honest!

Lyn Here –

Gets money from purse.

Have a ride on something else.

Ryan They're all shit.

Lyn Don't swear. Why don't you try *The Twirling Tea Cups*.

Ryan They're broke.

Gordy Wonky saucer.

Lyn There must be something worth having a ride on.

Gordy *Mysteries and Wonders.*

Lyn Eh?

Gordy (*at* **Ryan**) See that trailer right at the back? Painted gold?

Ryan . . . Yeah.

Gordy See what it says on the side?

Ryan . . . Er.

Lyn Just tell him.

Gordy 'Dare you enter . . . *Mysteries and Wonders?'*

Ryan What *Mysteries and Wonders*?

Gordy 'Roll up, roll up! Gasp at the fifty rats killed by getting all their tails tangled together! Wonder at the head of an albino crocodile! Touch a rock from the surface of Mars! Shiver at the sight of The Man with No Eyes.

Ryan No eyes?

Gordy A curse. From a gypsy. 'Your greedy eyes have led you to sin! I'll cover those eyes with skin, skin, skin!'

Lyn He don't wanna see stuff like that.

Ryan I do.

Lyn Well, I'm not giving you the money for it.

Takes money back.

Gordy Just say Gordy sent you.

Ryan Gordy?

Gordy Gordy.

Ryan *rushes off.*

Lyn If you smile at me one more time I'll knock some teeth out.

Gordy I love it when women talk rough.

Slight pause.

Lyn It was so . . . special once. This fair.

Gordy So they tell me.

Lyn The first year we moved here . . . there were posters for it everywhere. Everyone was so excited. 'A fair's coming! A fair!' When it arrived – oh, it was so bright. So colourful. The whole town turned out. Families. Now look at it . . . a few drunken kids and a freak show.

Gordy *Fake* show, you mean.

Lyn Eh?

Gordy I tied the rat tails myself. The crocodile's bleached. That rock from Mars? From Southend, I think – No. Dorset.

Lyn And the man with skin over his eyes?

Gordy I make it.

Lyn What?

Gordy The skin. I used to live with this make-up artist. She came to our school to give a careers talk. Life in the entertainment industry. I was only fifteen but we . . . we sort of hit it off. You know?

Lyn What your parents think of that?

Gordy Mum's dead. Dad's a drunk. Not much thinking from either of them. A neighbour – he sort of took me under his wing. He raced greyhounds. Anything you want to know about greyhounds, come to me.

Lyn Thank you. I will.

Slight pause.

Gordy They've let Ryan in *Mysteries and Wonders*.

Lyn I can see that – And don't say his name.

Gordy You know what happens to greyhounds when they stop winning races. They're killed. That was my job. I'd take them to the wood at the back of the stadium. I'd tie their leads round branches. Leave them to hang. Some of them would whimper and struggle for ages. One day I noticed people gathering nearby. Greyhound fans. Fuck, I thought, I'm in trouble now. But I wasn't. The people – they just wanted to watch. I invited them closer. Front-row seats. Next time I did it, word had spread. There were twice as many people. I charged them money. Every time I did it the audience grew. I made more money from killing the dogs than my neighbour did from racing them.

Pause.

Wanna meet later?

Lyn A candlelit dinner and advice on strangling dogs?

Gordy If that's what you want.

Ryan *walks up.*

Ryan It was all shit.

Lyn Don't swear – Let's go home.

Gordy What about The Man with No Eyes?

Ryan Worst fucking make-up I've ever seen.

Lyn Ryan!

Ryan *has walked off.*

Gordy There's a gold mask. In the *Mysteries and Wonders*. Supposed to be from the ancient Aztecs.

Ryan (*calling, off*) Mum!

Lyn Yes! Coming!

Gordy I made it. Out of gold foil and glass beads. The Aztecs used to believe gold was the . . . the excrement of the gods. The mask might be fake . . . but it still looks good. It can still give pleasure. No harm in that, is there?

Lyn . . . You know the old factory?

Gordy The car plant. I think so, yeah.

Lyn Tomorrow. Three-thirty. Main gate.

13

Office in factory. Day.

Ryan *alone.*

Jack (*off, calling*) Ryan!? . . . Ryan!?

Ryan Here!

Jack Where?

Ryan Office. Opposite the old water machine thing.

Jack *enters.*

Jack Fuck me. I've never actually been *in* the old car plant before – You sure it's safe?

Ryan Yeah.

Jack Don't wanna fall through the fucking floor and land on a mop handle and have it shoot up my arsehole and through my guts and pop out the top of my head or something.

Ryan Don't be stupid.

Jack It happened, mate! Some man in some place in America. Connecticut. He dressed up as Father Christmas. Him and his wife wanted to prove Santa exists to their kids. He's up on the roof. There's snow everywhere. His wife's filming. You can hear her laughing. Which sort of ruins the whole point of the exercise, but that's women for you. Then suddenly – the man slips. He slides off the roof. Whoosh! Below him, in the garden, there's this mop handle sticking straight up out of a bucket of frozen water. Bosh! The man lands right on it. Impaled. He's stuck there like a fucking scarecrow. He's still alive. It's at this point the wife – just to prove what a total shit-for-brains she is – stops filming. Can you believe it? Honestly, some people don't deserve a high-definition camera – Hey, is this the room where your mum . . . you know? When you were keeping watch outside.

Ryan . . . I think so, yeah.

Jack It's a lot tidier than I imagined. They could've fucked on the floor easy.

Ryan They don't fuck. Okay?

Jack Whatever – You see all the syringes and drug stuff on the stairs?

Ryan Yeah.

Jack I took a photo of it with this –

Reveals mobile phone.

Da-dahhh!

Ryan Thought your mum said you couldn't have another one.

Jack She needs me to have one, don't she. So she can call me to do stuff. 'Bring me home a kebab!' 'Come back and help me have a crap.'

Ryan You don't?

Jack What?

Ryan Help her have a crap.

Jack Well, no, I don't dig the shit out her arsehole with a spoon, if that's what you're thinking. But I help her get up the stairs to the toilet. She's so fucking heavy the toilet's coming away from the wall. She's like an elephant sitting on a fucking egg cup.

Phone rings.

It's her!

Answers.

Mum! Can't talk! They're after me again! Krafer and his gang. They're gonna kill me, Mum! They're gonna kill me!

Hangs up.

Ha, ha!

Ryan She'll be really worried now.

Jack Nah. She'll eat a cream doughnut.

Mobile rings.

Ryan Told you! She's worried!

Jack *answers mobile.*

Jack Don't phone, Mum! Please! I'm hiding! You're putting me at risk! I'm in danger, Mum! Big danger!

Hangs up.

Don't look at me like that, mate. You know what I've spent the morning doing? Washing her – and not her cunt and stuff before you ask. Just her back and legs and arms. Then I have to rub this *E45* cream into all her creases.

Ryan What creases?

Jack Her flab. The skin gets all sweaty and sore between the layers. She stinks like old trainers sometimes.

Ryan You shouldn't talk about your mum like that.

Jack Why not?

Ryan Cos . . . she's your mum.

Jack Oh . . . right.

Ryan . . . Drawing class!

Jack Eh?

Ryan You wanted to learn to draw, right?

Jack Fuck! Yeah. But first . . . I've got a little surprise for you.

Ryan I've got a surprise for you too, mate.

Jack Fuck! What?

Ryan Yours first, mate.

Jack No. Yours, mate.

Ryan Yours, mate.

Jack Yours, mate.

Ryan Yours, mate.

Jack Okay, okay . . . it's on the phone.

Ryan What?

Jack Your brother. See if you think it's a fake or not.

Slight pause.

Come on.

Ryan Fuck off.

Jack Ryan, mate, you have to see it sometime.

Ryan I don't.

Jack I'll just turn it on and –

Ryan You cunt. I'm going.

Heads for door.

Jack All right, all right.

Ryan . . . You won't play it.

Jack No.

Ryan Get rid of it, then.

Jack What?

Ryan Delete it.

Jack Later.

Ryan I'm not staying in the same place as . . . that.

Jack Okay, okay. Jesus. You get the arsehole so fucking quick, don't you.

Presses buttons on mobile.

Gone.

Ryan Promise?

Jack Yeah.

Ryan Okay.

Jack So . . . what's your surprise for me?

Slight pause.

Come on, mate.

Ryan . . . Okay.

Gets sketchbook from bag.

Da-dahhh!

Jack What is it?

Ryan A sketchbook.

Gives book to **Jack**.

Jack You mean . . . It's for me.

Ryan Yeah.

Jack Every page.

Ryan Yeah.

Jack Oh, mate. Mate!

Ryan And . . . these.

Gets pencils from bag.

Jack Pencils!

Ryan Coloured pencils.

Jack Mine to keep?

Ryan Yeah.

Jack Forever?

Ryan They won't last forever.

Jack Why not?

Ryan Cos you'll use fucking use them, won't you!

Jack Okay, okay . . . So! What we gonna draw, eh?

Ryan Okay . . . Lesson one.

Ryan *and* **Jack** *sit.*

Ryan Get a clean page in your sketchbook.

Jack Got it – Know what I'd like to draw? That fox we saw last night. The one that scared us half to fucking death.

Ryan We're gonna draw something much better.

Jack What?

Ryan An alien.

Jack From outer space?

Ryan Yeah.

Jack Fuck!

Ryan Take the black pencil, Jack.

Jack . . . Yeah, yeah.

Ryan Now draw a curvy line across the page . . . like this.

Jack . . . Yeah.

Ryan Now . . . do a curvy line under it . . . like this.

Jack Hang on, hang on, not too fast.

Ryan Sorry.

Jack . . . Like this?

Ryan Yeah. Now . . . At this end . . . do a line here . . . and here . . . put a dot right . . . here.

Jack Okay . . . Fuck, it's like a sort of snake's head.

Ryan Exactly.

Jack You mean . . . aliens look like snakes.

Ryan *Flying* snakes. The wings go . . . here. They're gold.

Jack What are?

Ryan The wings – I'll use yellow.

Colours in wings.

Jack How d'you know they look like this?

Ryan . . . I've seen them.

Jack When?

Ryan When we said goodbye to my brother.

Jack You mean aliens came to see him fucking buried?

Ryan My brother wasn't buried. He was cremated.

Jack Burnt.

Ryan Yeah.

Jack Why?

Ryan It's what he wanted. He left instructions. In case anything ever happened to him. He wanted to be cremated and his ashes put in fireworks.

Jack Fuck me.

Ryan He wanted them set off on top of Motorway Mound.

Slight pause.

Jack Well, go on, go on.

Ryan Eh?

Jack Aliens!

Ryan Oh! Well, Dad – he lit the fireworks. He told me, 'Stand back, Ryan! Fireworks can be dangerous, son!'

Jack He's right. I've seen a clip of when they go wrong. Nasty.

Ryan So I stood back and . . . Mum – she was a little further down the hill. She was crying so much she couldn't stand up. Our neighbours – they're holding her up. She's calling out my brother's name. 'Alec! . . . Oh, God! Alec! . . . Oh, God! Alec!' Over and over again. 'Oh, God! Alec!' Then – Bang! The whole sky explodes with colour. So bright. The fireworks light up all the whole hill. And . . . I look up and . . . I see them.

Jack Fuck.

Ryan They've left the safety of their ships and they're flying in and out of the fireworks . . . They're weaving in and out of the sparkling fire . . . Their wings are bright gold . . . And I start to feel so calm and . . . peaceful. Like everything's gonna be okay. I feel so happy. I start to laugh. Because I realise the aliens – they're talking to – Talking to me with feelings inside my head. They're saying, 'You are safe . . . you are safe . . .' I shout up at them, 'I am . . . I am . . . I am . . .'

Pause.

Ryan *touches* **Jack**'s *chest.*

Slight pause.

Jack What you doing?

Ryan . . . Dunno.

Slight pause.

Jack One of Krafer's mates – he used to play with my cock. I didn't mind. It was better than getting beat up . . . You wanna play?

Ryan . . . Okay.

Jack starts to undo belt on his jeans.

Jack Tell you what . . . you can do it on one condition.

Ryan What?

Jack Watch this.

Holds out mobile.

Ryan You said it was gone.

Jack I lied – Oh, come on.

Ryan No.

Jack Okay.

Goes to do belt up.

Ryan Wait!

Jack You'll watch?

Ryan . . . Yeah.

Jack It has to be *all* of it.

Ryan Okay.

Jack No backing out halfway through?

Ryan Okay, okay.

Jack *gives mobile to* **Ryan**.

Jack You ready?

Ryan No!

Pause.

Okay.

Jack *plays clip on mobile.*

Ryan *watches.*

We hear Alec say '. . . Monsters.'

Then . . .

Sound of Alec screaming etc.

Yells and shouts from his killers.

The sounds stop.

Silence.

Jack *takes mobile from* **Ryan**.

Jack Well?

Pause.

Fake or what?

Ryan . . . Looked real to me.

Jack Fuck me, mate, you blind?

Ryan It looked real. Okay? It looked real.

Jack Okay, okay, no need to get the arsehole again. Only a question, for fuck's sake. Okay . . .

Goes to undo jeans.

Ryan Don't.

Pushes **Jack**.

Jack *staggers back and falls.*

Jack Fuck me, no need for that, mate. Jesus.

Struggles to get up.

Help me up, mate . . . Come on . . . My bones are bending in this position – Shit! Shit!

Ryan *picks up brick.*

Jack Come on, mate.

Ryan *strikes* **Jack** *with brick.*

Jack Mate, what's that for? Come on!

Slight pause.

Ryan *strikes* **Jack** *again.*

Jack There's no need for – Mate! Don't!

Ryan *hits* **Jack** *some more.*

Jack *is screaming now.*

Jack Stop it, mate. It's fucking hurting . . . Don't! Mate! Let's do some drawing.

Ryan *continues to strike* **Jack**.

Jack Let's do . . . some drawing . . .

Screams fade.

Silence.

Jack *is still.*

Ryan *is still.*

Pause.

Ryan *drops brick.*

Slight pause.

Ryan *looks at the blood on his hands.*

He wipes his hands on **Jack**.

Ryan *covers* **Jack** *with sheets of hardboard etc.*

Slight pause.

Ryan *collects the sketchbooks and pencils.*

He starts putting everything in his bag.

He looks at the drawing **Jack** *had done.*

Slight pause.

A whimper starts to form in **Ryan***'s throat.*

He puts **Jack***'s sketchbook in his bag.*

Jack*'s mobile rings.*

Ryan*'s whimper gets louder.*

He stares at where **Jack** *is.*

Ryan*'s whimpering turns to crying.*

The mobile continues to ring.

Ryan *stares, unable to move, crying getting louder.*

Then –

Ryan *runs out.*

Fade to blackout.

Act Two

4

Hill top. Night.

Alec *is waiting.*

Camera and telescope etc. are set up.

Pause.

Mikey, *forties, approaches.*

Mikey Alec? What you doing up here, son?

Alec Forgot your sandwiches.

Mikey Oh . . . Thank you. Thank you.

Alec It's fine.

Mikey No, no. I appreciate it, son. Really.

Alec Dad, it's fine. Okay?

Mikey . . . You been waiting here long?

Alec A while.

Mikey Sorry, sorry.

Slight pause.

Alec You took a chance.

Mikey Eh?

Alec Leaving your stuff here.

Mikey Oh, no one up here this time of night. Just sad ol' sods like me. I saw something earlier, you know. Hovering above the factory. Purple light. Grabbed the camera but – Whoosh! Gone.

Alec . . . I saw you, Dad.

Mikey Eh?

Alec Going down the other side of the hill. The lorry in the lay-by.

Mikey Oh, that was ol' Jonny Follet. You remember Jonny. Used to be shop steward at the factory. His wife, Barbra, used to work in the canteen with your mum.

Alec I know who Jonny Follet is, Dad.

Mikey It was ol' Jonny who helped reopen the community centre for the J.D.C. meetings. Remember that first meeting, Al? The lights fusing. Scared us to bloody death. Bang! Ha, ha! Remember?

Alec I remember you called out, 'We're under attack! Take cover!'

Mikey I don't think I –

Alec You laughed. Everyone laughed. Because being shot at – that's one big joke, ain't it, Dad.

Mikey No, it's certainly not a –

Alec Bullets might cripple us or kill us, everyone, but –hey! – why the long faces? Where's your sense of humour? It's a joke. Laugh! Laugh!

Mikey Okay, son, okay.

Slight pause.

Alec . . . So good ol' Jonny's a lorry driver now, is he?

Mikey Well, it's a job son. He don't like it but . . . a steady wage. Self-respect, Al. You know? Besides, has its perks. If he's passing he sends me a text. 'Mikey! You up the hill looking for aliens, mate?' Ha, ha. We shoot the breeze about the good ol' days like the sad old sods we are – You're supposed to say, 'You're not a sad old sod, Dad!'

Slight pause.

Sandwiches! Fancy one?

Alec No.

Mikey What's on the menu tonight I wonder? Cheese 'n' cucumber? Tuna 'n' cucumber? . . . Chicken! Your mum's spoiling me tonight. It's because you're back home, you know. Oh, yes. I'll be getting caviar and champagne by the end of the week – Sure you don't want one?

Alec No, for fuck's sake, no.

Mikey Okay, son, okay.

Slight pause.

You know what I was thinking about earlier? The day we came up here to take the photo. What a day that was!

Alec How can I forget?

Mikey We'd only just moved here. Your mum – she was pregnant with Ryan. I said to her, 'Climb Motorway Mound in your condition? Are you mad, woman?' But you know your mum. Tell her not to do something, she'll want to do it all the more. It was the hottest day of the year. You remember that. Your mum nearly passed out when she reached the top. 'Liquids!' you said.

Alec I got her a drink.

Mikey You did, son. You remember helping me set up the tripod?

Alec One of the legs got stuck.

Mikey It still does.

Alec You put it over . . . here.

Mikey That's right. And I got you to stand there. Your mum beside you. The whole town – it was spread out behind you. The car plant. Rows and rows of gleaming cars.

Alec The fair had just arrived.

Mikey That's right, son. The fair. We could see them setting it up, couldn't we.

Alec You set the timer on the camera.

Mikey I rushed over to join you and your mum.

Alec The flash went off by mistake.

Mikey But we couldn't take another one – because . . .?

Alec Mum went into labour.

Mikey Panic! Ha, ha! What a day, eh?

Alec You were worried about losing your lens cap!

Mikey I was – ha, ha – I was.

They laugh.

Good memories, Al. Good memories.

Slight pause.

Alec . . . Guess who I bashed into yesterday.

Mikey Eh? What?

Alec Guess who. I bashed into. Yester. Day.

Mikey . . . Who, son?

Alec Dermot O'Driscoll.

Mikey Dermot? That rings a bell – Stan's son!

Alec Yeah.

Mikey Didn't ol' Dermot want to be a footballer?

Alec Years ago.

Mikey Not a multi-millionaire striker for Arsenal now then, is he?

Alec He weighs nineteen fucking stone, Dad.

Mikey Dermot O'Driscoll?! What happened?

Alec This place fucking happened.

Mikey . . . He got a job?

Alec Course he ain't got a fucking job.

Mikey It's his weight. He's lost his confidence. Now, you tell him to ring me and I'll –

Alec Oh, Dad, Dad.

Mikey I've got this number. You book to have a medical and if you're diagnosed as clinically obese you can –

Alec Just stop it, Dad, stop it.

Mikey I'm trying to help, son.

Alec Well, don't!

Slight pause.

Dermot and me – we went for a drink.

Mikey Oh, that's great.

Alec Why's that 'great', Dad? Eh?

Mikey . . . Where'd you go?

Alec New place at the back of where the cinema used to be.

Mikey Nice?

Alec It's a shit hole, Dad. The whole fucking town's a shit hole.

Mikey Well, I wouldn't say it's that bad exactly –

Alec I've seen carpet-bombed shanty-towns look more fucking inviting. Okay?

Slight pause.

Dermot's girlfriend was there.

Mikey Nice girl?

Alec Seemed okay.

Mikey What's she do?

Alec Clothes shop.

Mikey Enjoy it?

Alec Jesus, Dad – I don't fucking know. I didn't give her a questionnaire to fill in.

Slight pause.

She said there's an alleyway behind where she lives. She says it's become a sort of meeting place. Know what for?

Mikey What?

Alec Men.

Mikey Men?

Alec Men and men.

Mikey Oh. Well . . . ha, ha . . . it takes all sorts to make the world go round, son.

Alec You think it's funny, do you?

Mikey Well, it's not that I find it –

Alec Men who don't know each other. Strangers. Fucking over the car bonnets. Sucking each other's cocks.

Mikey But, son . . . if there's no one getting hurt –

Alec Ruckshana can see them from her bedroom window – And if you say Ruckshana's a lovely name, I'll fucking thump you one, Dad, I swear I will. Ruckshana says in the morning – This alleyway. This alleyway you see no harm in. It's full of used condoms. Hundreds. All over the pavement like . . . like squashed fucking . . . – Locusts. Locusts!

Slight pause.

Mikey What's all this about, son?

Alec How long's it been going on?

Mikey What?

Alec Flying saucers as a cover.

Mikey 'As a cov – '?

Alec For you sucking men's cocks.

Mikey Oh, Alec . . . No . . . no, you've got to stop all this . . . this . . .

Alec This? This?

Mikey You've had your mum in tears this week. Accusing her of . . . of flirting with your mates and Christ knows what else.

Alec She *did*!

Mikey She *didn't*, Al!

Alec I was fucking ashamed. She'd wear those short dresses and flash her knickers –

Mikey Jesus, Al, don't start it all again.

Alec We've got to face the truth, Dad. How else are we going to . . . to . . . – I *know* what Mum is like. My eyes are sand-blasted clean. I *see* her, Dad. It's like her skin is transparent and I can see all the . . . all the snakes and scorpions –

Mikey I won't let you talk like this about your –

Alec I've explained things to Ryan.

Mikey You've . . . what?

Alec He has a right to know. All Mum's airs and graces. How she was a secretary in some posh law firm before I was born –

Mikey She was!

Alec Her crucifixes and her classy clothes –

Mikey Classy! Yes!

Alec It's all a fucking act! She wanted my friends to slam her on the kitchen table and rape her.

Mikey Enough! Okay? Enough!

Starts packing up telescope etc.

Alec You could be hung from a crane.

Mikey Wh-what?

Alec For what you did. I've seen it. Two men. Teenagers. Their hands were tied behind their backs. There was a crane with two nooses attached to its arm. The nooses were put round the necks of the young men. Then the crane lifted its arm. You know what happens when you're hung like that? There's no snapping neck. No quick end. You dangle. You choke. Your face turns bright red. It swells up like it's gonna burst. Your eyes bulge like fucking billiard balls. You die slow, Dad. Real slow. There was a huge crowd watching. Some of them were just kids. And you know what? Everyone loved it. They cheered. They laughed. They jumped up and down with excitement. Fuck, perhaps some of them got turned on, Dad, what d'you think?

Mikey Jesus Christ, Al.

Alec It happens! Teenagers stoning pretty young girls to death. You think that ain't a turn-on? Eh? You think it's done purely out of a sense of religious fucking conviction? Don't make me laugh. And what about the beheadings, Dad. You watched any of those?

Mikey No!

Alec You should! I've seen hundreds. Masked men killing some poor sod. Know what it all looked like, Dad? A fucking homo gang-bang rape.

Mikey Stop it, Al.

Alec Men holding another man down. Holding him close. Real close. Feeling the warmth of his body. His heartbeat. His breath. And all the time the man's writhing and moaning, 'No, no.' And then they pull back his head. It's like they want to kiss him, Dad, I kid you not. The man's neck – it's exposed. You can see his veins throbbing. And then – A hard blade. The thrust. The penetration. The spurting.

Mikey I'm not listening.

Alec And who's to say they're wrong to do it? Eh? The beheadings. The stonings. The hangings. Who's to say it's . . . it's uncivilised and . . . and . . . Cos I tell you this – on that day. The day those men were hung. I stayed in that town. All day. And it was orderly and . . . and it was friendly. The people gave us food and they . . . the . . . the whole place . . . me being there . . . It felt clean! *Clean!* You know what I'm saying?

Mikey No!

Alec I mean I didn't see middle aged women sucking their son's friends' cocks or . . . or middle-aged men fucking each other in lorries and . . . and . . . I feel sick with the thought . . . sick with it . . .

Mikey Son . . .

Alec This place – It's over, Dad.

Mikey No, no, Alec. There's a new government initiative to regenerate the whole –

Alec I'm not talking about fucking Draylingstowe! Jesus! Your mind – it's so fucking . . . small. I'm talking about *everything*, Dad. *All* of us. This thing we call our fucking way of life. It's in the death throes. Don't you see that? It's kicking and gasping and struggling – but there's no more air. It's over. We're like . . . like dinosaurs bedazzled by all the pretty lights in the sky, too fucking stupid to realise it's a comet getting closer and closer . . . – And this way of life . . . this is what you want me to come back to, eh? This fucking . . . terminal illness – You'd rather I was here than back out there?

Mikey You promised your mum you wouldn't go back!

Alec I've got mates out there, Dad! Taz!

Mikey I know, son, but . . . Family, son!

Alec Taz – he's going back tomorrow.

Mikey Alec!

Alec I could go back with him!

Mikey Don't break your mum's heart, son.

Alec And yours, Dad? Eh? Will your heart be broken if I went back?

Mikey Of course it will.

Alec Then tell me what happened in the lorry.

Mikey Jesus Christ!

Alec Tell me! . . . *Tell me!*

Mikey I was just talking to Jonny Follet.

Alec Well, I don't fucking believe you.

Mikey . . . He's got cancer. Okay? He don't want anyone outside the family to know. Pancreatic. He's scared. He needs to talk. There. Happy now?

Slight pause.

Alec . . . Oh, Dad, Dad.

Mikey What?

Alec How can you lie about something like that?

Mikey I am not fucking lying, Alec. I wouldn't.

Alec I can go round and ask him.

Mikey Don't you dare.

Alec Cos it's a lie.

Mikey Because he told me in confidence.

Alec How fucking convenient.

Mikey Jesus!

Alec The truth, Dad! That's all I want. Is that too much to fucking ask? Eh? To come back to here and – just once! Once in a fucking lifetime – Have someone tell me something that is absolutely fucking true. Now, you tell me, Dad, or, I swear, I'm back in barracks by the morning.

Mikey . . . I don't . . . I don't know what you want me say.

Slight pause.

Alec *goes to walk away.*

Mikey Wait!

Alec *stops.*

Pause.

Mikey . . . I . . . had sex with another man.

Alec . . . Again.

Mikey I had sex with another man.

Slight pause.

Alec . . . *Did* you?

Slight pause.

Dad?

Mikey No . . . I talked to Jonny.

Alec Oh, Dad.

Mikey I had sex.

Slight pause.

I talked.

Slight pause.

Sex.

Slight pause.

Talk.

Slight pause.

Sex . . .

8

Kitchen. Day.

Ryan *is sitting at a table, drawing.*

Slight pause.

Lyn *enters, wearing dressing gown.*

Lyn What you doing indoors?

Slight pause.

You need to go outside and make some friends.

Slight pause.

What you drawing?

Ryan Nothing.

Lyn *potters round kitchen.*

Ryan *continues drawing as –*

Lyn You know why I stopped taking you to school? I was ashamed. I'd look at all the other mothers with their sons. Their healthy boys. What have I got left?

Ryan Me.

Lyn You.

Slight pause.

No wonder your dad's run away. Why would he want to stay? You're not going to amount to anything. You're not exactly hero material, are you? Who'd ever want to build a statue in memory of you.

Ryan No one.

Slight pause.

Lyn What if there was a fire? Eh? One of the wires in the telly sets fire to the curtains. What if it happened while I was in bed? Fast asleep. Smoke creeps up the stairs. I'm knocked unconscious. Would you be able to save me?

Ryan I shouldn't think so.

Slight pause.

Lyn You eaten anything?

Ryan Yeah.

Lyn What?

Ryan I finished the Jaffa cakes.

Lyn We've got cornflakes.

Ryan There's no milk.

Lyn Buy some.

Ryan No money.

Lyn You know where my purse is.

Ryan No money in your purse.

Lyn There must be enough for a pint of milk.

Ryan No.

Lyn . . . What if masked men break into the house? Eh? They're holding guns. Would you be able to save me? With your little crippled hands?

Ryan You wouldn't *want* me to help.

Lyn I wouldn't?

Ryan You'd probably arranged the whole thing. They're probably Alec's old school friends. The ones you fancied so much. You told them what time to turn up and what to wear and everything. It'd turn you on.

Lyn You think so?

Ryan You'll see me standing over there and you'll give me that look of yours.

Lyn And what look's that?

Ryan 'Fuck off, Ryan, Mum's busy.'

Lyn Oh, *that* look.

Ryan Yeah. *That* look. You love it when the first man's cock goes in you. You grab hold of him. You have lots of orgasms one after the other. You tell the others to fuck you. They fuck you up the cunt and up your arse and in your mouth and . . . and your ears –

Lyn My ears?

Ryan Yes! They fuck your ears! They fuck every fucking hole they can. They fuck you and fuck you fuck you and you love every fucking minute of it. You tell them to spunk all over you. It's all in your hair and dribbling down your legs. It's like . . . like a fucking dinosaur's sneezed all over you.

Pause.

Lyn *takes pencil from* **Ryan**.

Slight pause.

Lyn *presses tip of pencil on table.*

The lead breaks.

Slight pause.

Ryan *picks up another pencil and starts drawing.*

Slight pause.

Lyn *takes pencil from* **Ryan**.

Slight pause.

Lyn *presses tip of pencil on table.*

The lead breaks.

Slight pause.

Ryan *picks up another pencil and starts drawing.*

Slight pause.

Lyn *takes pencil from* **Ryan**.

Then she takes all the other pencils.

One by one, **Lyn** *breaks the lead in all of them.*

Pause.

Ryan *opens his pencil box and gets out sharpener.*

He starts sharpening a pencil.

Lyn *starts crying.*

Slight pause.

Ryan *goes to* **Lyn**.

He holds her.

2

Community hall. Night.

A 'JUSTICE FOR DRAYLINGSTOWE CHILDREN' banner.

The hall is in darkness, a photo projected.

Mikey *is talking into a microphone.*

Mikey These are the hands of Ryan, my own son. Ryan is nearly ten years old now. This photo was taken when he was still a toddler – before numerous operations to try and correct the defects – and, as you can see, most of Ryan's fingers on both hands are joined together. There are also several small bones either missing or fused together. Ryan is also severely short-sighted. No operation has been able to correct that.

Another photo.

Now this . . . this is little Maisy. Maisy is the daughter of my good friends and neighbours, Cheryl and Ravi. Now, I'd like to say Maisy was the same age as my son but I can't cos our little Maisy here died when she was just five months old, a matter of days after this photo was taken – Okay, lights, Jonny, please, mate!

The lights come on.

And, everyone, can we all put our hands together to show our appreciation for good ol' Jonny Follet who went to a great deal of trouble getting this community centre opened for this – our first J.D.C. meeting here tonight. Thank you, Jonny!

Claps.

Okay . . . now for the facts. And I'm not gonna embellish anything cos – as those of you who know me from the ol' factory days will testify – I am not one of your flowery types. So . . . the town of Draylingstowe rose from the marshy wastelands of Essex roughly twenty years ago, primarily to service the ever-expanding Draylingstowe car plant which had, at that time, just been taken over by the Japanese company, Karura, all genuflect and Hail Mary. At that time the cars produced were the Model T Karura, the Roadster Karura and the Sedan Karura. About ten years ago, that's when I moved my family here – along with five hundred other families, all part of the West Side housing development, also known as the Motorway Sound Muffler Scheme, very funny, I'm sure – two new models were introduced to the factory production line – the Escort and the Deluxe – and, with them, a whole new range of specially created Karura colours. The most popular of these colours was known professionally as RX 12111 Series Four metallic finish, commonly known as – Showroom Stan'll know this . . . Phoenix Sun! So what's the problem, I hear you ask? A popular car with a popular colour. Well, the problem, brothers and sisters – though none of us knew it at the time, not us poor workers at any rate – was that this RX 12111 Series Four was poison. Yes! Poison! The car company's own tests proved the paint could have, and I quote, 'detrimental health issues'. And what connects that with all the photos we've just seen? I'll tell you! All those poor babies and children were born or conceived during that two-year period when the poison paint was being used, that's what! Coincidence? You think so? Eh? . . . No! And nor do I!

Slight pause.

Now . . . now, before I go on, I want to make one thing clear. This has nothing to do with what happened after the events I've just described – namely, Karura deciding it was no longer profitable to have a car plant here and just fucking off back to the land of the rising sun – excuse my French, ladies – leaving all of us here, stranded in total bloody darkness. No! This has nothing to do with sour grapes – or should that be polluted saki – but it has *everything* to do with our children! With our children's future! With justice!

Points at banner.

'Justice for Draylingstowe Children!' J.D.C.! And we – the J.D.C. brothers and sisters – we will win. We *will* get justice. Why? Because we – the J.D.C. – we would do anything for our children. Wouldn't we? Eh? Anything – And while we're on the subject of children – indulge me, indulge me – can I just mention my eldest, Alec, who is about to go off to serve his country. He's here with us tonight and I'm sure you'd all like to show him you're as proud of him as I am – Come up, Alec . . . Come on, son . . .

Alec *joins* **Mikey** *on stage.*

Alec *is in uniform.*

Mikey Don't he look smart? A man in uniform, ladies? Eh? – *Draylingstowe Gazette*? Wakey-wakey!

Camera flashes.

Mikey Say a few words son.

Alec Oh . . . I dunno . . .

Mikey Come on. Don't be shy.

Alec Well . . . I'd just like to say . . . my dad's the greatest bloke I know.

Mikey *and* **Alec** *embrace.*

The lights fuse with a loud bang.

Mikey *and* **Alec** *jump.*

Mikey We're under attack everyone. Ha, ha, ha. Take cover! Take cover!

15

Hospital waiting room. Day.

Evie *is asleep in a chair.*

Gordy *approaches.*

Slight pause.

Gordy Hello.

Evie *doesn't wake.*

Gordy Excuse me.

Touches **Evie**.

Evie Oh!

Gordy I'm sorry.

Evie Everything's alright now, don't you worry about a thing . . . Where is this?

Gordy . . . The hospital.

Evie Will you let me think for a moment, please.

Slight pause.

I'm sorry. They gave me some tablets to . . . to . . . What's the time?

Gordy About ten.

Evie Night?

Gordy Morning.

Evie . . . You're the one who found my son.

Gordy How d'you know?

Evie You told me.

Gordy I ain't said a word.

Evie Oh, you don't have to use words. Not with Evie. Let me look at you . . . Oh, you poor lamb. Just a child yourself. What's your name, hon?

Gordy Gordy.

Evie Gordon. The patron saint of . . .

Gordy I don't think it *is* a saint.

Evie Some obscure one, I think – You're an Aries.

Gordy Capricorn.

Evie I thought so – Gordon! The patron saint of saving children's lives. That's it!

Gordy He's gonna live then?

Evie Eh?

Gordy Your son.

Evie Oh, he's gonna be just fine.

Gordy I thought he was dead when I found him.

Evie Oh, you poor thing – Sit down. Tell Evie all about it. Come on.

Gordy *sits.*

Gordy I went to the old car plant . . .

Evie Drugs was it, hon?

Gordy Eh?

Evie Why you were in the car plant.

Gordy Er . . . Yeah.

Evie I thought so. You didn't have any on you when the police –

Gordy Oh, no, no.

Evie Cos it would break my heart, hon, it would, I swear, if you got in trouble for drugs just cos you gave my son a helping hand when he was down on his luck – Oh, these bloody seats! Hospitals! Why can't they put a cushion on them or something.

Gordy . . . I heard his phone.

Evie Eh?

Gordy Your son's phone started to ring.

Evie That was me calling, I bet. Don't tell me it was the sound of my ringing led you to my little Jack.

Gordy Whoever did it to him . . . they'd tried to cover him up. To hide what they did. I lifted the stuff off him. There was blood. I could see the bone of his skull – I shouldn't be telling you this.

Evie Don't you worry about me. I'm as tough as an old ox. Face like one too, my son says – ha, ha!

Gordy There's something else.

Slight pause.

When I was there . . . kneeling beside him . . . he grabbed my finger. Like a baby does. You know? The rest of his body . . . nothing moved. His eyes stayed closed. Everything was covered in dust. He was like one of those figures in Pompeii. You know? After the volcano. Your son's grip – it was so tight. Like he was clinging on to . . . to life. I said, 'Don't worry. I won't leave you . . . I won't leave you . . .'

Evie Now, you listen to me. My Jack's gonna be just fine. They've operated on him and he's . . . on this machine or something and –

Gordy Machine?

Evie It's normal, hon.

Gordy Normal? A machine?

Evie What d'you fucking want me to say? Eh? That I'm shit scared? I am! You want me to run around like a fucking headless whatsit . . . and . . .? – They tried to kill my son. Those murdering bastards. I know who they are. *Everyone* knows. That Krafer kid from the estate and his bunch of vicious – My son phoned me when they were chasing him. He was so scared. 'Krafer and his gang are gonna kill me, Mum!' That's what he said. 'I'm in danger!' He was hiding from them. Like something hunted. But they found him. And they . . . they . . . – Can you get me drink, hon, I'm a bit parched all of a sudden. There's a machine over there.

Gordy I don't think I've got any . . . any change.

Evie Where's my bag?

Gordy Here.

Gives handbag to **Evie**.

Evie I'll have some chocolate if anything's going. Milk. No nuts.

Gets money from purse and gives it to **Gordy**.

Gordy What do you want to drink?

Evie Oh . . . Coke. Diet.

Gordy *goes to machine.*

He gets drink. Then –

Gordy There's no chocolate.

Evie What kind of hospital is this?

Gordy *returns with drink and gives it to* **Evie**.

He watches her drink.

Pause.

Gordy How long you gonna stay here?

Evie Well, they promised to get me a taxi but –

Gordy I'll get you a taxi. I'll make sure you get home okay. Have you got any food in the house?

Evie . . . Some.

Gordy We'll get something on the way.

Evie Why, what a . . . caring human being you are.

Gordy I try to be.

Evie I feel that, yes.

Gordy What else do you feel, Evie? Tell me.

Slight pause.

Evie . . . Hold my hand.

Gordy *holds* **Evie***'s hand.*

Evie Oh, yes . . . Mmm . . . Some sadness . . .

Gordy Yeah.

Evie Years ago . . . many years . . . When you were a child.

Gordy I was eight.

Evie That's right. You were eight. I see that clearly. I see . . . a figure . . . Close to you . . . Loving . . . Your loving father . . . Mother! Yes! . . . She's got a message for you . . . She says . . . She's sorry . . . She's sorry she . . . left . . . died . . . killed herself . . . She says you mustn't think it was your fault. She didn't do it because of anything *you* did. She says it was just . . . her depression . . . her illness . . . Your father . . . His drink . . . His violence . . . Yes. Your father's violence towards her and you . . . It was all too much . . . She wants you to know she still loves you. Her arms are still around you. And they will be around you for always.

Gordy So . . . you're a medium or something, are you?

Evie Evie the Miraculous – mystic, medium, spiritual healer, fortune teller, guru for the Google generation.

Gordy People can make a fortune at that game.

Evie It's not a game, hon.

Gordy What is it, then?

Evie . . . It's a gift.

3

Ryan's room. Night.

Ryan *is showing* **Alec** *photos on a laptop.*

Ryan Now this . . . this was taken in Arizona on the thirteenth of March 1997, brov. This is a very famous incident.

Alec *looks at photo.*

Alec Lights in the sky.

Ryan In a perfect 'V' shape!

Alec Helicopters fly in that formation.

Ryan Helicopters!? This was seen over Arizona and Nevada and the Mexican state of . . . Snore.

Alec Snore?

Ryan Something like that. This V-shaped object that made no noise and it –

Alec Whoah, whoah, what 'V-shaped object'? It's a bunch of lights.

Ryan It's a huge V-shaped UFO! Look!

Alec Mmm . . . well . . .

Ryan People saw the straight lines of the edge of the craft – Here! . . . You see?

Alec Er . . . No, brov.

Ryan Well, me and a billion other people in the world can.

Alec It's called 'illusory contours'.

Ryan What is?

Alec When you see several things – lights like this – and your eye sort of . . . makes connections. Joins them up. Sees unifying shapes where there are none. Like when people look at the stars and see the Plough or Pegasus or something.

Ryan . . . Sonora.

Alec What?

Ryan The Mexican state.

Alec You're not listening to me.

Ryan This is a quote from Mr Bill Greiner. He saw the V-shaped object. 'I'll never be the same again.' – That's an American accent, by the way.

Alec I gathered.

Ryan 'Before this, if anyone has told me they saw a UFO, I would've said, "Yeah, and I believe in the tooth fairy." But now I've got a whole new view. I may be just a dumb truck driver, but I've seen something that was not of this world.' You hear that, Al? 'Something that was not of this world'. Guess how long the V-shaped object hovered above him?

Alec Ooo . . . two minutes and twenty-two seconds?

Ryan An hour!

Lyn (*calling, off*) Alec!

Ryan Mum wants you.

Alec I know – Go on.

Slight pause.

Go on.

Ryan . . . Now, Dad – he recorded this clip from the hill top seven weeks ago. It's daytime, as you can see. It's a bit blurred –

Alec Like most of Dad's stuff.

Ryan There! Above the factory. Five objects. In what shape?

Lyn (*calling, off*) Alec!

Alec I don't see any shape, brov.

Ryan A *V*-shape!

Alec It just looks like a . . . bunch of balloons.

Lyn (*calling, off*) Alec?

Alec Hang on! Seven weeks ago. August?

Ryan Yeah.

Alec The fair would be in the park, right? . . . Right?

Ryan . . . Might've been.

Alec Don't these look like shiny fairground balloons to you, Ryan? Be honest.

Ryan No. They bloody don't. Fairground balloons don't fly in a perfect bloody V-shape from one side of Draylingstowe to the other – Look! You can see them moving! You think Dad's up on that hill wasting his time taking photos of stupid balloons? Dad says this area's a 'hot spot'. Know what that means? Extra-terrestrials come here a lot. Which is more than I can say for some fucking *people* I know.

Lyn (*calling, off*) Al?

Ryan He's in here!

Lyn *opens bedroom door.*

Lyn . . . Everything okay, boys?

Alec Fine.

Lyn (*at* **Alec**) I didn't know if you'd gone out or not, love.

Alec Well, I'm out at the moment but I might be back any minute now.

Slight pause.

Lyn . . . Your dad's forgotten his sandwiches. Thought you might like to take them up to him.

Alec *doesn't react.*

Slight pause.

Lyn I'll take them if you're busy with your brother.

Alec No, no, I'll take them, Mum.

Lyn . . . Good boy.

Ryan I'll go too.

Lyn It's past your bedtime.

Ryan I'm not tired.

Lyn School in the morning. No.

Ryan But Mum –

Alec Just do as you're fucking told!

Slight pause.

Lyn *puts sandwiches down.*

Lyn Your Aunt Becky phoned. I told her you said you weren't going back. She said her prayers have been answered. I said, yours and mine.

Alec Ooo, the power of prayer, eh, Mum? Aunt Becky firing off in Australia. You letting loose here. Poor God didn't stand a chance, did He. No wonder He made me say I wasn't going back. Which is odd because, when I joined, I seem to remember you and Aunt Becky being pretty sure *that* was God's will too.

Slight pause.

Lyn . . . It's turning chilly. I'd put your coat on, if I were you.

Lyn *leaves.*

Pause.

Ryan It's okay, Al. If you shout and stuff.

Alec It is?

Ryan Yeah. Dad explained.

Alec What did he explain?

Ryan That you've . . . seen stuff.

Alec What stuff?

Ryan . . . Out there. It's made you . . . You know.

Alec No. What?

Slight pause.

What's it made me?

Slight pause.

What's it made me?

Slight pause.

Wanna see some photos?

Takes mobile from pocket.

Ryan . . . Yeah. Great.

Looks at photo on mobile.

What's that?

Alec Sandstorm.

Ryan It's all yellow.

Alec That's what sandstorms are like. You can see it coming towards you. Like a big yellow tsunami. The sand goes everywhere. Down your throat. Ears. Up your nose.

Ryan Can it kill you?

Alec If you ain't got protection it can – Here! Look!

Goes to another photo.

Ryan That you?

Alec It's Taz.

Ryan Your best mate, right?

Alec Right. And you see all that stuff he's wearing – I wear it too. No way sand can hurt us. It still turns our spit yellow though.

Ryan Ugh!

Alec And snot. It goes rock hard. If I sneeze – a bullet.

Ryan Your secret weapon!

Alec Surrender or I'll snot you!

Ryan I surrender! I surrender!

They both laugh.

Ryan *continues looking through photos.*

Ryan Who's that?

Alec Taz again. His tattoo.

Ryan Snakes?

Alec Yeah.

Ryan Another one of Taz. He sunbathing?

Alec Yeah.

Ryan In a war?!

Alec We have time off, you know.

Ryan Taz again . . . Again – You both going swimming or something?

Alec Give it here.

Takes mobile from **Ryan**.

Look at this one – See?

Ryan Who's that?

Alec An old woman.

Ryan She looks pissed off.

Alec We had to search her village for weapons.

Ryan You think *she's* got weapons?

Alec What did I tell you?

Ryan 'Trust no one'.

Alec Exactly.

Another photo.

Ryan Where's that?

Alec Inside the woman's house.

Ryan There's you! In the mirror. You see?

Alec . . . The woman's screaming behind me. Waving her arms in the air. Spitting and stuff. Taz is trying to calm her down. The walls of the room are all cracked. There's a framed photo. It's of her ten-year-old boy. It must be her son. His face is all . . . smiling and happy. I'm looking at his smiling face and listening to his mum scream. The translator is telling her we're not going to hurt her. I walk out of the room. The hallway is quite dark. I walk down it. The old woman's screams get quieter. The walls are cracked. It gets darker. I see a door at the end of the corridor. Something's shining on it. Gold. It's the door knob. I walk closer. I reach out and I grab hold of the gold . . . Careful . . . My gun's at the ready . . . I open the door . . . It's dark inside . . . I step forward. The window has been boarded over. I hear breathing. Whimpering. And then I see it. On a mattress in the corner of the room.

Ryan What?

Alec *shows photo.*

Ryan What . . . what *is* it?

Alec The woman's son.

Ryan Is he alive?

Alec Yeah. He's been injured.

Ryan By a bomb?

Alec No. Well . . . yes *and* no. Some bombs landed nearby. An oil lamp or something fell on the boy. He went up like a Roman candle.

Ryan It looks like he's . . . he's all melted.

Alec They got him to hospital. There were no drugs or anything.

Ryan No painkillers?

Alec No.

Ryan But . . . he must've been in a lot of pain and –

Alec I know, Ryan, I know.

Ryan So . . . what did the doctors *do*?

Alec Put some bandages on.

Ryan That all?

Alec That's all.

Ryan But . . . couldn't *you* do anything?

Alec What could *I* do, Ryan?

Ryan I . . . I dunno. Perhaps you could . . .

Alec What?

Slight pause.

Perhaps I could *what*?

Ryan . . . I dunno.

Slight pause.

Alec When I first saw him . . . laying there like that . . . know what I thought it was?

Ryan What?

Alec . . . An alien.

7

Lyn's living room. Night.

Lyn *is sitting on armchair.*

Mikey *enters.*

Mikey He's asking for you.

Slight pause.

He can hear breathing again.

Slight pause.

I said you'd go up.

Slight pause.

Lyn?

Lyn Alright.

Mikey *sits and starts going through papers and photos etc.*

Lyn *watches him.*

Pause.

Ryan (*calling, off*) Mum!

Slight pause.

(*Calling, off.*) Mum!

Mikey (*calling*) Mum's just on the phone to your Aunt Becky, son! She won't be long.

Slight pause.

Continues to go through papers etc.

Lyn *continues watching.*

Pause.

Lyn Mr Busy . . . Busy-Busy . . .

Slight pause.

Mikey'*s mobile rings.*

Mikey It's Taz!

Answers mobile.

(*Into mobile.*) Taz, how are you, mate? . . . Oh, don't you worry about us, mate, we're bearing up. What about you . . . – Now, you stop right there, soldier, and you listen to your ol' Uncle Mikey, okay? Alec would not have wanted you to be feeling like this, you know that don't you. What happened to Alec was the worst thing in the world, mate, but it was just bad luck.

Lyn 'Bad luck'?

Mikey Alec was in the wrong place at the wrong time. That's all. There's no . . . no meaning behind it, Taz . . . There's no significance in it being him and not you. We just have to move on. We have to find a way of getting out of bed every morning and looking the future in the face and saying, 'Bring it on.'

Lyn 'Bring it on'!?

Mikey So let me . . . let me tell you some developments that've been happening at this end, soldier, that okay with you? . . . Good . . . First, the charity we're setting up in Alec's name to help support families of soldiers lost in battle is going great guns.

Lyn Jesus!

Mikey We're calling it F.A.R.U.F. . . . *Friends and Relatives United Forever*. What d'you think?

Lyn It's a bloody joke.

Mikey What else to report? – Oh, yes! The *Draylingstowe Gazette* is doing a big article next week and – wait for this, mate, wait – it looks like they're gonna get fully behind my idea to have a statue of Alec on Motorway Mound as a sort of cenotaph for our own little community and –

Lyn *snatches mobile from* **Mikey**.

She cuts off call.

Mikey What you – ? That was Taz!

Lyn I know who it fucking was.

Mikey He's concerned about us.

Lyn He's concerned about himself.

Mikey No, no.

Mobile rings.

Lyn *answers it.*

Lyn (*into mobile*) You should be dead!

Mikey Don't, Lyn!

Lyn *and* **Mikey** *struggle over phone.*

Mikey Give it to me . . . No!

Lyn Alec took your fucking place that day. Why were you sick? Why did you stay in barracks? It should've been you ambushed on that fucking road. It should've been you who was fucking kidnapped and –

Mikey *gets mobile from her.*

Mikey (*into mobile*) Taz? . . . Mate?

Slight pause.

He's gone.

Lyn Good.

Ryan *has rushed into room.*

Ryan Dad?

Mikey Go back to bed, Ryan.

Goes to dial on mobile.

Lyn Don't you *dare* call him back.

Mikey It's not Taz's fault, Lyn.

Goes to leave room.

Lyn I said, don't you fucking dare –

Lyn *grabs* **Mikey**.

They struggle over mobile.

Ryan *tries to separate them.*

Ryan Don't . . . Stop it . . . Mum . . .

Lyn *gets phone from* **Mikey**.

Mikey Taz had a fever, Lyn. You know that. Some insect. You might as well blame the fucking insect for what happened to – Go back to bed, son. Everything's alright.

Lyn 'Everything's alright'? No! Everything is *not* fucking alright! Our son was butchered –

Mikey Lyn.

Lyn It was filmed. *Filmed!*

Mikey Get out, Ryan.

Lyn People watch it. Millions of people. They watch it for fun. They leave comments. Comments! – What did you say to him on that hill?

Mikey Oh, please, Lyn, don't start that again.

Lyn He wasn't going to go back. He *promised* me.

Mikey I know.

Lyn And then he comes back from you and – He's packing his bags! What happened?

Mikey Nothing happened!

Lyn *points at* **Ryan**.

Lyn *You* said something!

Ryan Dad?

Mikey Jesus, Lyn, leave the boy alone!

Lyn *grabs hold of* **Ryan**.

Lyn He was in your room before he went up there.

Ryan Dad?

Lyn What did you say to him? What did you say?

Mikey You fucking bitch! You bitch!

Tries to pull **Lyn** *away from* **Ryan**.

All three of them struggle.

The struggle gets increasingly violent.

Some furniture and ornaments are knocked over.

Much screaming and overlapping of dialogues etc.

Then –

Mikey *hits* **Lyn**.

They all freeze.

Silence.

Pause.

Mikey Go upstairs, please, son.

Ryan *does not move.*

Mikey Do as you're fucking told! Do it! Do it!

Ryan *runs upstairs.*

Pause.

Mikey Men we have never met took our son. They took him without our express permission. They tortured him then they . . . killed him. And there is no understanding it. There is no meaning. No coming to terms with it. Not now. Not tomorrow. Not ever. We will wake up every day for the rest of our lives and we will breathe razor blades and we will swim through bleach. And there is no escape from this.

There is no comfort. There is just . . . blades and bleach. Until we die.

Very long pause.

Lyn *goes upstairs.*

Slight pause.

Ryan *enters.*

Slight pause.

Ryan . . . Dad?

Slight pause.

Dad?

Mikey Oh . . . hello, son. So . . . we've still gotta sort out that pesky breathing sound upstairs, haven't we?

Ryan . . . Yeah.

Mikey *starts tidying the room.*

Mikey You know what I think it is? A draught coming down the air shaft.

Ryan *starts picking up some things.*

Ryan *holds up a framed photo.*

Ryan The frame's broke.

Mikey Oh . . .

Ryan Will it stick back?

Mikey Yeah, yeah. Easy. You know in some places – ancient China, I think – they used to fill the cracks on broken things with gold.

Ryan Really?

Mikey Oh, yeah. They wouldn't try to hide the bits that were damaged or missing. Just the opposite. They thought the missing bits were more . . . were more . . . precious . . .

Weeps.

Ryan *watches.*

17

Evie's living room.

Jack *is in wheelchair.*

Evie *is showing off new dress.*

Evie What d'you think, hon? . . . It's not too young for me, is it? The girl in the shop said it was my colour and everything – Oh, she was so helpful, hon. Her name was Ruckshana – ain't that a lovely name. I said to her, 'Ruckshana, if I had a little daughter I would name her that, I really would.' – Shoes!

Goes to shopping bags.

Can you believe how pretty all the shops make their bags now, hon. I said to Ruckshana, 'Shana, this shop's bag is such a work of art. I'm never gonna throw it away.' Shana says, 'They're all like that now.' I tell her, 'Well, Shana, it's been many a long year since I've been brave enough to walk into a shop like this and try clothes on.' And she says to me, 'Well, why's that, Evie,' and then . . . well, I told her, hon. Told her how big I used to be. Oh, the look on pretty Shana's face. She couldn't believe it – Da-dahhh!

Holds shoes in air.

What d'you think? . . . Not too tarty, are they? Shana said they were made for this dress.

Puts shoes on.

Oh, I'd forgotten how it felt to wear high heels. The tightness you get in your legs here. Oh, hon, you know what wearing these is like? It's like going back in time, it really is. This tightening is making me remember the world as it used to be. You know? Running to catch a bus . . . going to the hairdressers . . . not being afraid of mirrors and – Oh! The handbag, hon!

Gets handbag.

Shana said that this was her favourite handbag but she couldn't afford it. I said to her, 'You should get your boyfriend to buy it for you, hon.' And you know what she told me? Her poor boyfriend is a very depressed young man. I asked Shana why. She said, 'I think it's his weight, Evie. You see, he weighs . . .' And the poor girl couldn't even say it, hon. She could not get the words out of her mouth. I said to her, 'Shana, it's a pretty sad state of affairs when a girl's unable to say how much her own boyfriend weighs.' She leant real close and whispered it in my ear. Honestly, you'd think she was telling me the location of the Ark of the Covenant. I said, 'Shana, hon, twenty-two stone ain't the end of the world.' She says, 'But he wanted to be a footballer when he was younger, Evie. All his dreams are gone now.' And that's when I realised. I was sent into the shop for a reason. I said, 'Shana, I can help your boyfriend.' And I told her, hon. About you and what you can do for people. I said, 'Shana, my Blessed Jack is a channel through which all the positive energy of the universe is channelled and intensified. Through him all things are healed and made right. The face of Jesus appeared as stigmata on his back.' And I showed her the photograph of that miracle, hon. I said, 'Shana, I have seen old women, crippled with arthritis, throw away their zimmer frames and dance the rumba after coming into contact with my Jack. He's a Lourdes on wheels. He can cure anything – including obesity, hon. Why, I'm living proof of that, am I not? You tell your boyfriend to make contact with me and you'll be snuggling up to a footballer with a six pack before you can say . . . whatever.' I gave her our card, hon. Oh, I do hope we're hearing from that poor fat boy very soon cos I won't sleep at night knowing he's wobbling about out there, cos I know how it –

Mobile rings.

Hon! That's him now. I just know it.

Gets mobile.

Why, it's Kieran Follet –

Answers mobile.

Kieran, my sweet lamb, how are you? . . . Mmm . . . Oh, hon, I can feel your mum's sadness coming right down the line and hitting me in the face like a wet haddock – Jack, it's our lovely friend Barbra. She's taken to her bed with depression again . . . Oh, Kieran, can you hear this? The Blessed Jack is already sending out a Jack Blessing all the way across Draylingstowe to your house – Listen, hon!

Holds phone out.

There, Kieran, you hear? . . . Of course we can come round to see you tomorrow. House calls are our speciality now at no added expense to you. I'm sure when I make contact with your dad your mum will feel – What? . . . Then what is it brought on the depression, hon? . . . Well, I did hear about that, yes, but I assumed it was just one of those drug addicts . . . Oh, no . . . No, hon, don't say that . . . Well, yes, I did know him . . . well, when I say 'know' I mean I offered my help after he and his wife lost their son in that horrible way but they were not inclined to – What's that? Well, yes, I've got the paper, but I haven't had a chance to – Oh, okay, hon. You go to your mum. She needs you. See you tomorrow.

Hangs up.

Oh, Jack, I've just had some very distressing news . . .

Gets newspaper from bag.

Yes! Here . . . Oh . . . Oh, hon, listen to this, 'The badly decomposed body that was found hanging in a locked room in the basement of the derelict Draylingstowe car plant has now been identified as Michael Tyler. Michael – known as 'Mikey' to his friends – came to Draylingstowe ten years ago when the car plant was expanding and invested in . . .' Blah, blah . . . Oh, hon, hon . . . It says they think the body's been there all this time. Since the day he left home . . . Oh . . . Listen to this, 'The only personal possession found on him was an old family photograph taken on top of Motorway

Mound. It has been revealed by the family that, before killing himself, Mikey Tyler had written the word "Monsters" three times on the back of the photograph. These were the last words spoken by his son Alec just before he was beheaded' – oh, it's too terrible, hon, too terrible . . . It says here his wife and youngest son Ryan are emigrating to start a new life with Mrs Tyler's sister in Australia.

Jack *is getting increasingly agitated.*

Evie Hon? . . . What's wrong? . . . Oh, don't do this to me. I'm upset enough as it is.

Sound of front door opening etc.

Gordy (*calling, off*) It's only me!

Evie Thank God!

Gordy *enters.*

Gordy (*at* **Evie**) Well, what have we here? A glamour model no less – Kiss me, beautiful.

Embraces and kisses her.

Evie No, Gordy, no – Jack!

Gordy Jesus.

Rushes to **Jack**.

Gordy What's wrong, sunshine . . . It's okay, it's okay – Evie! Valium!

Evie *hesitates.*

Gordy The valium, for fuck's sake! Come on!

Evie *gives tablets to* **Gordy**.

Gordy Don't worry, Jack . . . calm down now.

Gives tablet to **Jack**.

Gordy What did you do to him?

Evie Nothing! – Just talking.

Gordy Well, don't! (*At* **Jack**.) Shhh now . . . There's nothing to worry about . . . Gordy's here . . . Gordy's here . . .

Jack *is calming.*

Evie If it makes you feel better to pick on me, then do it.

Gordy Eh – ? Oh, Evie, I didn't mean to –

Evie Evie's place is in the wrong.

Gordy Look out the window.

Evie What?

Gordy Go on.

Evie *looks out of window.*

Evie . . . What?

Gordy *jangles car keys.*

Gordy Surprise, surprise.

Evie No!

Gordy Yes!

Evie *That* car!

Points outside.

Ours?

Gordy Ours!

Evie But we . . . oh, we can't afford it.

Gordy We *can*. We *have*.

Evie Oh, I love you, I love you.

Kisses **Gordy**.

Gordy I love you too, beautiful.

Evie Oh, Jack, hon. We've got us a beautiful car. It's all gold and shiny.

Gordy Let's have a spin, eh?

Evie A spin! – You hear that, hon?

Gordy Straight down the motorway – fast as a bullet! Come on!

Heads for front door.

Evie A spin! A spin!

Rushes after him.

Jack *is alone.*

Sounds of delight can be heard as **Evie** *gets a closer look at the car.*

Jack *makes noises.*

Gordy *rushes back in, followed by* **Evie**.

Gordy I thought you were bringing him.

Evie I got carried away – Sorry, hon!

Gordy Come on, sunshine.

Evie Spin!

Gordy Motorway!

Evie Bullet!

Gordy Lightspeed!

Evie *and* **Gordy** VROOMMM!!

They push **Jack** *outside.*

1

Hill top. Day.

Alec, *twelve (played by the actor playing* **Ryan**), *rushes on, carrying bag.*

Mikey *and* **Lyn** *follow.*

Lyn *is heavily pregnant.*

Alec You see the view? Look! – Mum!?

Mikey You okay, Lyn?

Lyn Don't worry about me.

Alec Fluids! That's what you need.

Lyn Yes. A drink. Thank you, Alec.

Alec *gets a bottle of water from bag.*

Mikey Said it was too hot for you, didn't I.

Alec He did, Mum.

Lyn Boys, boys. Women in Africa plough fields in my state.

Mikey They don't plough up a hill, love.

Lyn Just set the camera up.

Alec *gives water to* **Lyn**.

Lyn Oh, thank you.

Mikey Alec! Tripod!

Alec Tripod!

Goes to bag.

Lyn Oh, look at that view!

Alec I told you. Great, eh? You can see the whole town – Dad!

Gives tripod to **Mikey**.

Lyn Everything looks so . . . sparkling. So clean.

Alec See our house?

Lyn . . . Yes! Oh, we *have* to get a lawn in our garden . . . Mikey!?

Mikey I know, I know.

Lyn Look at Cheryl's. It's all green.

Mikey Cheryl and Ravi've been here since April, love.

Struggling with tripod.

This bloody leg . . .

Lyn You do it, Al. We'll be here all day.

Mikey *I* can do it.

Lyn Just let him have a go, love.

Mikey *gives tripod to* **Alec**.

Lyn See all those cars, Mikey?

Mikey Eh?

Lyn The factory – Look!

Alec I'm gonna work in the factory, ain't I, Dad?

Mikey If that's what you want, son.

Lyn Golden insects.

Mikey What?

Lyn Squint . . . The cars. Rows of golden beetles or something.

Mikey Phoenix Sun.

Lyn Eh?

Mikey The colour. Wanna know its professional name?

Lyn No.

Alec I do, Dad.

Mikey RX 12111 Series Four metallic finish.

Lyn How d'you remember all this stuff?

Mikey It's my job.

Lyn He knows everything about the cars except how to drive one.

Mikey I'll pass the test next time – You'll see!

Lyn He'll back into another car, more like.

Alec Another twenty-point turn.

Mikey That's enough, you two.

Alec Done it!

Indicates tripod.

Mikey Mr Universe.

Alec Camera, Dad?

Mikey Camera, son!

Alec *gets camera from bag.*

Lyn What's happening in the park down there?

Mikey Eh –? Oh, that must be the fair.

Lyn Of course, yes.

Alec Can I go Mum?

Lyn We can *all* go – Dad?

Mikey Family night out.

Alec Yesss!

Lyn Oww!

Touches stomach.

Now, *there's* a kick.

Alec Ryan wants to go to the fair too.

Mikey Fancy that, love? Once round the rollercoaster?

Lyn I'll give it a miss this time.

Alec Pregnant women in Africa would do it.

Mikey Ha! – Very good!

Lyn Shut up and talk to your brother.

Indicates belly.

Alec We're on the hill beside the motorway, Ryan – You sure he can hear me?

Lyn Of course he can hear you.

Mikey Babies start hearing at seven months.

Alec He don't understand what I'm saying, though, does he.

Lyn He understands you want him and love him – Right, Dad?

Mikey Tell him it's the hottest day of the year so far, Al.

Alec It's the hottest day of the year so far, Ryan. The sky – it's all blue.

Lyn Not a cloud.

Alec We've come here so Dad can take a photo of us.

Mikey Tell him his mum wants to send it to his Auntie Becky in Australia.

Lyn That's not the *only* reason.

Mikey Oh, yes it is.

Lyn It's not. But . . . well, if Becky is going to see our new home I'd like her to see it when everything's at its best. The grass on the hill is so green – Make sure you get the green hill in, Mikey.

Mikey I will, I will.

Lyn . . . Who'd have thought it, eh?

Mikey What's that, love?

Lyn Us. The way it's all worked out.

Mikey We've been lucky, that's for sure.

Lyn Oh, it's more than just luck. Come on.

Mikey Take cover, Alec. I feel a 'god moment' coming on.

Lyn But it *has* to be more than just . . . chance. Well, don't it? Be honest now.

Alec Any good, Dad?

Indicates camera.

Mikey Not sure . . .

Lyn What made me get on the wrong bus that day? Eh?

Mikey Perhaps she'd been on the Bacardi Breezers, eh, Al?

Alec Yeah. You got on the wrong bus cos you were tipsy, Mum. Ha!

Lyn I'm *serious*, you two. And when I got off the bus . . . why'd that woman come up and ask me where Hackney Town Hall was? 'They're building five hundred new homes in Draylingstowe,' she said. 'There's a model of what it'll all look like. You can put your name down if you're interested. Come on.' And that look in her eyes . . .

Mikey What you saying, Lyn? A guardian angel led you to a new home in Draylingstowe?

Alec Ha, ha!

Lyn Why not? – Don't laugh, Alec. God's looking after us.

Mikey Okay, okay, that's enough.

Lyn What's wrong with saying that?

Mikey What's wrong – ? It's superstitious claptrap, Lyn.

Lyn *That* from the man who went looking for the Loch Ness Monster.

Mikey I got a photo! Alec's seen it.

Alec It's the monster, Mum.

Lyn It's driftwood. *Driftwood!*

The camera starts working.

Mikey Okay . . . we have life!

Lyn You see?

Mikey It's a charged battery, love, not a resurrection.

Lyn Don't, Mikey. Please.

Mikey Okay, okay – Now . . . stand there . . . That's it. Alec – you here . . . Closer together.

Sets timer on camera.

Don't forget to smile!

Lyn All I'm trying to say is . . . we can't just be . . . hurtling through nothing . . . towards nowhere – Can we?

Mikey Keep still.

Camera flashes as –

Lyn Oww!

Clutches stomach.

Mikey Jesus!

Alec Was it meant to flash, Dad?

Mikey No!

Goes to camera.

Alec Let's do it again.

Lyn Oh! Mikey!

Alec Mum?

Lyn I'm fine, I'm fine, don't worry – Mikey!

Mikey Eh? What?

Lyn Ryan!

Mikey What? Now?

Lyn Yes. Very much now.

Mikey Okay, okay. Right. Okay. So . . .

Lyn You'll phone Ravi.

Mikey Yes. That's it. I'll phone Ravi. He can . . . he can –

Lyn Meet us at the bottom of the hill.

Mikey That's it. He can meet us and . . .

Lyn Drive us straight to the –

Mikey The hospital! I know, I know.

Lyn Oww!

Alec Mum!

Lyn I'm fine, I said. Women in Africa – Oww!

Mikey *is dialling on mobile.*

Mikey Alec! The stuff, son!

Indicates camera.

Alec Yeah, yeah.

Starts packing stuff away.

Mikey Can you walk okay?

Lyn Course I can bloody walk.

Mikey *and* **Lyn** *are walking off.*

Mikey Don't forget the lens cap, Al!

Lyn Lens cap!? You're worried about the bloody *lens cap*!?

Alec *looks for lens cap.*

Mikey (*into mobile*) Cheryl, it's Mikey. Is Ravi there please, love? . . . Ravi! It's the moment, mate . . . Yeah . . . We're on Motorway Mound. Can you meet us at the bottom and – ? . . . That'll be great, great.

The voices of **Mikey** *and* **Lyn** *are getting fainter and fainter as they disappear.*

Lyn (*calling, off*) Alec!

Alec Coming, Mum.

Continues looking for lens cap.

Lyn (*calling, off*) Alec . . . Come on, Alec . . .

Light fades to become night and –

6

Hill top. Night.

The actor playing **Alec** *puts on glasses and now becomes –*

Ryan *standing alone.*

Lyn*'s cries now become those of a mother at her son's funeral.*

Lyn (*calling, off*) Alec! . . . Oh, God! Alec! . . .

Oh, God! Alec! . . . *etc.*

Mikey (*calling, off*) Stand back, Ryan! Fireworks can be dangerous, son!

Ryan *steps back and looks up at the sky as –*

Fireworks explode!

The lights of the fireworks are bright and colourful.

Ryan *watches as his brother's funeral fireworks fizz and explode.*

Then **Ryan** *seems to see something amongst the fireworks.*

He smiles with joy and excitement.

The lights get brighter.

Ryan*'s smile gets bigger and bigger.*

He starts to laugh.

Ryan I am . . . I am . . . I am . . .

Blackout.